50 Italian Risotto Variation Recipes for Home

By: Kelly Johnson

Table of Contents

- Classic Risotto Milanese
- Lemon and Asparagus Risotto
- Mushroom and Thyme Risotto
- Tomato and Basil Risotto
- Truffle Infused Risotto
- Spinach and Parmesan Risotto
- Seafood Risotto
- Butternut Squash Risotto
- Saffron Risotto
- Pumpkin and Sage Risotto
- Gorgonzola and Walnut Risotto
- Roasted Red Pepper Risotto
- Pesto Risotto
- Shrimp and Pea Risotto
- Artichoke and Lemon Risotto
- Tomato and Mozzarella Risotto
- Radicchio and Balsamic Risotto
- Smoked Salmon Risotto
- Zucchini and Lemon Risotto
- Porcini Mushroom Risotto
- Roasted Vegetable Risotto
- Sun-Dried Tomato Risotto
- Lobster Risotto
- Spring Vegetable Risotto
- Ricotta and Spinach Risotto
- Beetroot and Goat Cheese Risotto
- Lemon and Mint Risotto
- Caramelized Onion and Gouda Risotto
- Broccoli and Cheddar Risotto
- Brown Butter and Sage Risotto
- Burrata and Cherry Tomato Risotto
- Eggplant and Tomato Risotto
- Pomegranate and Feta Risotto
- Green Pea and Pancetta Risotto
- Wild Mushroom Risotto

- Lemon and Dill Risotto
- Leek and Gruyère Risotto
- Fig and Prosciutto Risotto
- Roquefort and Pear Risotto
- Champagne Risotto
- Walnut and Gorgonzola Risotto
- Sage and Pumpkin Risotto
- Arugula and Pine Nut Risotto
- Orange and Almond Risotto
- Pecorino and Black Pepper Risotto
- Basil and Pine Nut Risotto
- Blue Cheese and Pear Risotto
- Smoked Trout Risotto
- Walnut and Cranberry Risotto
- Buttermilk and Lemon Risotto

Classic Risotto Milanese

Ingredients:

- 1 1/2 cups Arborio rice
- 1/2 cup dry white wine
- 4 cups vegetable or chicken broth, kept warm
- 1 small onion, finely chopped
- 2 tablespoons unsalted butter
- 2 tablespoons olive oil
- 1/2 cup Parmesan cheese, grated
- A pinch of saffron threads
- Salt and pepper, to taste

Instructions:

Infuse Saffron:
- In a small bowl, soak the saffron threads in 2 tablespoons of warm water. Allow it to infuse while you prepare the risotto.

Prepare Broth:
- Heat the vegetable or chicken broth in a separate saucepan and keep it warm over low heat.

Sauté Onion:
- In a large, heavy-bottomed skillet or pan, heat 1 tablespoon of butter and 1 tablespoon of olive oil over medium heat. Add the finely chopped onion and sauté until translucent.

Toast Rice:
- Add the Arborio rice to the skillet and cook for about 2 minutes, stirring constantly, until the rice is lightly toasted.

Deglaze with Wine:
- Pour in the dry white wine, stirring continuously until the wine is mostly absorbed by the rice.

Begin Adding Broth:
- Start adding the warm broth, one ladle at a time, to the rice. Stir frequently and allow the liquid to be absorbed before adding more.

Infuse Saffron:
- About halfway through cooking, add the saffron-infused water to the risotto, continuing to add broth and stirring.

Continue Cooking:
- Repeat the process of adding broth and stirring until the rice is creamy and cooked to al dente, usually around 18-20 minutes.

Finish with Butter and Parmesan:
- Remove the skillet from heat. Stir in the remaining 1 tablespoon of butter, 1 tablespoon of olive oil, and grated Parmesan cheese. Mix until well combined.

Season and Serve:
- Season the risotto with salt and pepper to taste. Allow it to rest for a minute before serving.

Garnish (Optional):
- Garnish with additional Parmesan cheese and a pinch of saffron threads if desired.

Serve Warm:
- Serve the Classic Risotto Milanese warm, enjoying the rich saffron-infused flavor and creamy texture.

This dish captures the essence of Northern Italian cuisine with its simplicity and luxurious taste. It can be enjoyed as a side dish or as a main course.

Lemon and Asparagus Risotto

Ingredients:

- 1 1/2 cups Arborio rice
- 1/2 cup dry white wine
- 4 cups vegetable broth, kept warm
- 1 bunch asparagus, trimmed and cut into bite-sized pieces
- 1 small onion, finely chopped
- 2 cloves garlic, minced
- Zest of 1 lemon
- Juice of 1 lemon
- 1/2 cup Parmesan cheese, grated (optional for a non-vegan version)
- 2 tablespoons unsalted butter or olive oil
- Salt and pepper, to taste
- Fresh parsley, chopped (for garnish)

Instructions:

Prepare Asparagus:
- Blanch the asparagus pieces in boiling water for 2-3 minutes until they are bright green and slightly tender. Immediately transfer them to ice water to stop the cooking process. Set aside.

Warm Broth:
- Heat the vegetable broth in a saucepan and keep it warm over low heat.

Sauté Onion and Garlic:
- In a large, heavy-bottomed skillet or pan, heat 1 tablespoon of butter or olive oil over medium heat. Add the finely chopped onion and sauté until translucent. Add the minced garlic and cook for an additional 1-2 minutes until fragrant.

Toast Rice:
- Add the Arborio rice to the skillet and cook for about 2 minutes, stirring constantly, until the rice is lightly toasted.

Deglaze with Wine:
- Pour in the dry white wine, stirring continuously until the wine is mostly absorbed by the rice.

Begin Adding Broth:

- Start adding the warm broth, one ladle at a time, to the rice. Stir frequently and allow the liquid to be absorbed before adding more.

Incorporate Lemon:
- When the rice is almost cooked, add the lemon zest and lemon juice to the risotto, continuing to add broth and stirring.

Finish Cooking:
- Continue adding broth and stirring until the rice is creamy and cooked to al dente, usually around 18-20 minutes.

Fold in Asparagus:
- In the last few minutes of cooking, fold in the blanched asparagus pieces.

Finish with Butter and Parmesan:
- Remove the skillet from heat. Stir in the remaining 1 tablespoon of butter or olive oil and grated Parmesan cheese (if using). Mix until well combined.

Season and Serve:
- Season the risotto with salt and pepper to taste. Allow it to rest for a minute before serving.

Garnish and Serve:
- Garnish with fresh parsley and additional lemon zest if desired. Serve the Lemon and Asparagus Risotto warm.

Enjoy the bright and vibrant flavors of this lemon and asparagus risotto, perfect for a light and refreshing meal.

Mushroom and Thyme Risotto

Ingredients:

- 1 1/2 cups Arborio rice
- 1/2 cup dry white wine
- 4 cups vegetable broth, kept warm
- 1 pound (about 450g) mixed mushrooms (e.g., cremini, shiitake, oyster), cleaned and sliced
- 1 small onion, finely chopped
- 2 cloves garlic, minced
- 2 tablespoons olive oil
- 2 tablespoons unsalted butter
- 1 tablespoon fresh thyme leaves, chopped
- 1/2 cup Parmesan cheese, grated (optional for a non-vegan version)
- Salt and pepper, to taste
- Fresh parsley, chopped (for garnish)

Instructions:

Sauté Mushrooms:
- In a large, heavy-bottomed skillet or pan, heat 1 tablespoon of olive oil over medium heat. Add the sliced mushrooms and cook until they release their moisture and become golden brown. Remove half of the mushrooms and set them aside for later use.

Prepare Mushroom Broth:
- In the same pan, add the remaining 1 tablespoon of olive oil and chopped onion. Sauté until the onion is translucent. Add minced garlic and cook for an additional 1-2 minutes.

Toast Rice:
- Add the Arborio rice to the pan and cook for about 2 minutes, stirring constantly, until the rice is lightly toasted.

Deglaze with Wine:
- Pour in the dry white wine, stirring continuously until the wine is mostly absorbed by the rice.

Begin Adding Broth:
- Start adding the warm vegetable broth, one ladle at a time, to the rice. Stir frequently and allow the liquid to be absorbed before adding more.

Incorporate Thyme:

- When the rice is almost cooked, add the chopped thyme to the risotto, continuing to add broth and stirring.

Finish Cooking:
- Continue adding broth and stirring until the rice is creamy and cooked to al dente, usually around 18-20 minutes.

Fold in Mushrooms and Butter:
- In the last few minutes of cooking, fold in the sautéed mushrooms that were set aside. Stir in the butter until well combined.

Finish with Parmesan:
- Remove the skillet from heat. If desired, stir in the grated Parmesan cheese.

Season and Serve:
- Season the risotto with salt and pepper to taste. Allow it to rest for a minute before serving.

Garnish and Serve:
- Garnish with fresh parsley and additional thyme leaves if desired. Serve the Mushroom and Thyme Risotto warm.

Enjoy the rich and earthy flavors of this mushroom and thyme risotto, a perfect dish for mushroom lovers and those who appreciate a savory, aromatic meal.

Tomato and Basil Risotto

Ingredients:

- 1 1/2 cups Arborio rice
- 1/2 cup dry white wine
- 4 cups vegetable broth, kept warm
- 2 large ripe tomatoes, diced
- 1 small onion, finely chopped
- 2 cloves garlic, minced
- 2 tablespoons olive oil
- 1/2 cup fresh basil leaves, chopped
- 1/2 cup Parmesan cheese, grated (optional for a non-vegan version)
- Salt and pepper, to taste
- Balsamic glaze (optional, for drizzling)
- Fresh basil leaves (for garnish)

Instructions:

Prepare Tomatoes:
- Dice the ripe tomatoes and set them aside.

Warm Broth:
- Heat the vegetable broth in a saucepan and keep it warm over low heat.

Sauté Onion and Garlic:
- In a large, heavy-bottomed skillet or pan, heat the olive oil over medium heat. Add the finely chopped onion and sauté until translucent. Add minced garlic and cook for an additional 1-2 minutes until fragrant.

Toast Rice:
- Add the Arborio rice to the pan and cook for about 2 minutes, stirring constantly, until the rice is lightly toasted.

Deglaze with Wine:
- Pour in the dry white wine, stirring continuously until the wine is mostly absorbed by the rice.

Begin Adding Broth:
- Start adding the warm vegetable broth, one ladle at a time, to the rice. Stir frequently and allow the liquid to be absorbed before adding more.

Incorporate Tomatoes:
- When the rice is almost cooked, fold in the diced tomatoes, continuing to add broth and stirring.

Finish Cooking:
- Continue adding broth and stirring until the rice is creamy and cooked to al dente, usually around 18-20 minutes.

Fold in Basil:
- In the last few minutes of cooking, fold in the chopped fresh basil. Stir until well combined.

Finish with Parmesan:
- Remove the skillet from heat. If desired, stir in the grated Parmesan cheese.

Season and Serve:
- Season the risotto with salt and pepper to taste. Allow it to rest for a minute before serving.

Garnish and Serve:
- Optionally, drizzle balsamic glaze over the risotto and garnish with fresh basil leaves. Serve the Tomato and Basil Risotto warm.

Enjoy the burst of freshness and the aromatic combination of tomato and basil in this delightful risotto. It's a perfect dish for the summertime when tomatoes and basil are at their peak flavor.

Truffle Infused Risotto

Ingredients:

- 1 1/2 cups Arborio rice
- 1/2 cup dry white wine
- 4 cups vegetable or chicken broth, kept warm
- 1 small onion, finely chopped
- 2 cloves garlic, minced
- 2 tablespoons truffle-infused olive oil
- 1/2 cup dry white wine
- 1/2 cup Parmesan cheese, grated (optional for a non-vegan version)
- Salt and pepper, to taste
- Fresh chives or parsley, chopped (for garnish)

Instructions:

Warm Broth:
- Heat the vegetable or chicken broth in a saucepan and keep it warm over low heat.

Sauté Onion and Garlic:
- In a large, heavy-bottomed skillet or pan, heat the truffle-infused olive oil over medium heat. Add the finely chopped onion and sauté until translucent. Add the minced garlic and cook for an additional 1-2 minutes until fragrant.

Toast Rice:
- Add the Arborio rice to the skillet and cook for about 2 minutes, stirring constantly, until the rice is lightly toasted.

Deglaze with Wine:
- Pour in the dry white wine, stirring continuously until the wine is mostly absorbed by the rice.

Begin Adding Broth:
- Start adding the warm broth, one ladle at a time, to the rice. Stir frequently and allow the liquid to be absorbed before adding more.

Continue Cooking:
- Continue adding broth and stirring until the rice is creamy and cooked to al dente, usually around 18-20 minutes.

Finish with Truffle Oil:

- Stir in additional truffle-infused olive oil to intensify the truffle flavor. Adjust the quantity according to your preference.

Finish with Parmesan:
- Remove the skillet from heat. If desired, stir in the grated Parmesan cheese.

Season and Serve:
- Season the risotto with salt and pepper to taste. Allow it to rest for a minute before serving.

Garnish and Serve:
- Garnish with fresh chives or parsley. Serve the Truffle Infused Risotto warm.

This truffle-infused risotto is an indulgent dish that brings the luxurious aroma and taste of truffles to the forefront. It's perfect for special occasions or when you want to treat yourself to a gourmet experience.

Spinach and Parmesan Risotto

Ingredients:

- 1 1/2 cups Arborio rice
- 1/2 cup dry white wine
- 4 cups vegetable or chicken broth, kept warm
- 4 cups fresh spinach, chopped
- 1 small onion, finely chopped
- 2 cloves garlic, minced
- 1/2 cup Parmesan cheese, grated (plus extra for serving)
- 2 tablespoons unsalted butter
- 2 tablespoons olive oil
- Salt and pepper, to taste
- Lemon zest (optional, for added freshness)
- Fresh basil or parsley, chopped (for garnish)

Instructions:

Warm Broth:
- Heat the vegetable or chicken broth in a saucepan and keep it warm over low heat.

Sauté Onion and Garlic:
- In a large, heavy-bottomed skillet or pan, heat 1 tablespoon of butter and 1 tablespoon of olive oil over medium heat. Add the finely chopped onion and sauté until translucent. Add the minced garlic and cook for an additional 1-2 minutes until fragrant.

Toast Rice:
- Add the Arborio rice to the skillet and cook for about 2 minutes, stirring constantly, until the rice is lightly toasted.

Deglaze with Wine:
- Pour in the dry white wine, stirring continuously until the wine is mostly absorbed by the rice.

Begin Adding Broth:
- Start adding the warm broth, one ladle at a time, to the rice. Stir frequently and allow the liquid to be absorbed before adding more.

Incorporate Spinach:

- When the rice is halfway cooked, add the chopped spinach to the risotto. Continue adding broth and stirring.

Finish Cooking:
- Continue adding broth and stirring until the rice is creamy and cooked to al dente, usually around 18-20 minutes.

Finish with Parmesan and Butter:
- Remove the skillet from heat. Stir in the grated Parmesan cheese and the remaining 1 tablespoon of butter. Mix until well combined.

Season and Serve:
- Season the risotto with salt and pepper to taste. If desired, add lemon zest for a burst of freshness.

Garnish and Serve:
- Garnish with additional Parmesan cheese and chopped fresh basil or parsley. Serve the Spinach and Parmesan Risotto warm.

This risotto is not only creamy and satisfying but also packed with the goodness of fresh spinach. Enjoy it as a comforting meal or a side dish for your favorite protein.

Seafood Risotto

Ingredients:

- 1 1/2 cups Arborio rice
- 1/2 cup dry white wine
- 4 cups seafood or vegetable broth, kept warm
- 1/2 cup dry vermouth or additional white wine
- 1 pound (about 450g) mixed seafood (shrimp, scallops, mussels, calamari), cleaned and prepared
- 1 small onion, finely chopped
- 2 cloves garlic, minced
- 2 tablespoons olive oil
- 2 tablespoons unsalted butter
- 1/2 cup Parmesan cheese, grated (optional for a non-vegan version)
- Salt and pepper, to taste
- Fresh parsley, chopped (for garnish)
- Lemon wedges (for serving)

Instructions:

Warm Broth:
- Heat the seafood or vegetable broth in a saucepan and keep it warm over low heat.

Prepare Seafood:
- If using mussels, make sure they are cleaned and debearded. For shrimp, peel and devein. If using calamari, clean and slice into rings.

Sauté Seafood:
- In a large, heavy-bottomed skillet or pan, heat 1 tablespoon of olive oil over medium-high heat. Sauté the seafood until cooked through. Remove the seafood from the pan and set it aside.

Sauté Onion and Garlic:
- In the same pan, add another tablespoon of olive oil. Add the finely chopped onion and sauté until translucent. Add the minced garlic and cook for an additional 1-2 minutes.

Toast Rice:
- Add the Arborio rice to the pan and cook for about 2 minutes, stirring constantly, until the rice is lightly toasted.

Deglaze with Wine:

- Pour in the dry white wine and dry vermouth, stirring continuously until the wine is mostly absorbed by the rice.

Begin Adding Broth:
- Start adding the warm seafood or vegetable broth, one ladle at a time, to the rice. Stir frequently and allow the liquid to be absorbed before adding more.

Incorporate Seafood:
- When the rice is halfway cooked, add the sautéed seafood back to the pan. Continue adding broth and stirring.

Finish Cooking:
- Continue adding broth and stirring until the rice is creamy and cooked to al dente, usually around 18-20 minutes.

Finish with Butter and Parmesan:
- Remove the skillet from heat. Stir in the remaining 1 tablespoon of butter and the grated Parmesan cheese (if using). Mix until well combined.

Season and Serve:
- Season the risotto with salt and pepper to taste.

Garnish and Serve:
- Garnish with fresh chopped parsley. Serve the Seafood Risotto warm, with lemon wedges on the side.

Enjoy the rich and savory flavors of the sea in this delightful seafood risotto. It's a perfect dish for special occasions or when you want to treat yourself to a gourmet meal.

Butternut Squash Risotto

Ingredients:

- 1 1/2 cups Arborio rice
- 1/2 cup dry white wine
- 4 cups vegetable broth, kept warm
- 2 cups butternut squash, peeled and diced
- 1 small onion, finely chopped
- 2 cloves garlic, minced
- 2 tablespoons olive oil
- 2 tablespoons unsalted butter
- 1/2 cup Parmesan cheese, grated (optional for a non-vegan version)
- Salt and pepper, to taste
- Fresh sage leaves, chopped (for garnish)

Instructions:

Warm Broth:
- Heat the vegetable broth in a saucepan and keep it warm over low heat.

Prepare Butternut Squash:
- Peel, seed, and dice the butternut squash into small cubes.

Sauté Butternut Squash:
- In a large, heavy-bottomed skillet or pan, heat 1 tablespoon of olive oil over medium-high heat. Add the diced butternut squash and cook until it is slightly caramelized and tender. Remove half of the squash and set it aside for later use.

Sauté Onion and Garlic:
- In the same pan, add another tablespoon of olive oil. Add the finely chopped onion and sauté until translucent. Add the minced garlic and cook for an additional 1-2 minutes.

Toast Rice:
- Add the Arborio rice to the pan and cook for about 2 minutes, stirring constantly, until the rice is lightly toasted.

Deglaze with Wine:
- Pour in the dry white wine, stirring continuously until the wine is mostly absorbed by the rice.

Begin Adding Broth:

- Start adding the warm vegetable broth, one ladle at a time, to the rice. Stir frequently and allow the liquid to be absorbed before adding more.

Incorporate Butternut Squash:
- When the rice is halfway cooked, add the sautéed butternut squash back to the pan. Continue adding broth and stirring.

Finish Cooking:
- Continue adding broth and stirring until the rice is creamy and cooked to al dente, usually around 18-20 minutes.

Finish with Butter and Parmesan:
- Remove the skillet from heat. Stir in the remaining 1 tablespoon of butter and the grated Parmesan cheese (if using). Mix until well combined.

Season and Serve:
- Season the risotto with salt and pepper to taste.

Garnish and Serve:
- Garnish with the reserved caramelized butternut squash cubes and chopped fresh sage.

Enjoy the warm and comforting flavors of butternut squash in this delicious risotto. It's a perfect dish for the fall or any time you want a hearty and satisfying meal.

Saffron Risotto

Ingredients:

- 1 1/2 cups Arborio rice
- 1/2 cup dry white wine
- 4 cups chicken or vegetable broth, kept warm
- 1 small onion, finely chopped
- 2 cloves garlic, minced
- 2 tablespoons unsalted butter
- 2 tablespoons olive oil
- 1/2 cup dry white wine
- A pinch of saffron threads (about 1/4 teaspoon)
- 1/2 cup Parmesan cheese, grated (optional for a non-vegan version)
- Salt and pepper, to taste
- Fresh parsley, chopped (for garnish)

Instructions:

Warm Broth with Saffron:
- In a small bowl, soak the saffron threads in 2 tablespoons of warm water. Allow them to infuse while you prepare the risotto. Add the saffron-infused water to the warm broth.

Sauté Onion and Garlic:
- In a large, heavy-bottomed skillet or pan, heat 1 tablespoon of butter and 1 tablespoon of olive oil over medium heat. Add the finely chopped onion and sauté until translucent. Add the minced garlic and cook for an additional 1-2 minutes.

Toast Rice:
- Add the Arborio rice to the pan and cook for about 2 minutes, stirring constantly, until the rice is lightly toasted.

Deglaze with Wine:
- Pour in the dry white wine, stirring continuously until the wine is mostly absorbed by the rice.

Begin Adding Broth:
- Start adding the warm saffron-infused broth, one ladle at a time, to the rice. Stir frequently and allow the liquid to be absorbed before adding more.

Continue Cooking:

- Continue adding broth and stirring until the rice is creamy and cooked to al dente, usually around 18-20 minutes.

Finish with Butter and Parmesan:
- Remove the skillet from heat. Stir in the remaining 1 tablespoon of butter and the grated Parmesan cheese (if using). Mix until well combined.

Season and Serve:
- Season the risotto with salt and pepper to taste.

Garnish and Serve:
- Garnish with chopped fresh parsley. Serve the Saffron Risotto warm.

Savor the exquisite flavor and luxurious color of saffron in this classic risotto. It's a perfect side dish for special occasions or a comforting meal on its own.

Pumpkin and Sage Risotto

Ingredients:

- 1 1/2 cups Arborio rice
- 1/2 cup dry white wine
- 4 cups vegetable or chicken broth, kept warm
- 1 cup pumpkin puree
- 1 small onion, finely chopped
- 2 cloves garlic, minced
- 2 tablespoons olive oil
- 2 tablespoons unsalted butter
- 1/2 cup Parmesan cheese, grated (optional for a non-vegan version)
- 8-10 fresh sage leaves, chopped
- Salt and pepper, to taste
- Roasted pumpkin seeds (optional, for garnish)

Instructions:

Warm Broth:
- Heat the vegetable or chicken broth in a saucepan and keep it warm over low heat.

Sauté Onion and Garlic:
- In a large, heavy-bottomed skillet or pan, heat 1 tablespoon of butter and 1 tablespoon of olive oil over medium heat. Add the finely chopped onion and sauté until translucent. Add the minced garlic and cook for an additional 1-2 minutes.

Toast Rice:
- Add the Arborio rice to the pan and cook for about 2 minutes, stirring constantly, until the rice is lightly toasted.

Deglaze with Wine:
- Pour in the dry white wine, stirring continuously until the wine is mostly absorbed by the rice.

Begin Adding Broth:
- Start adding the warm vegetable or chicken broth, one ladle at a time, to the rice. Stir frequently and allow the liquid to be absorbed before adding more.

Incorporate Pumpkin Puree:

- When the rice is halfway cooked, stir in the pumpkin puree. Continue adding broth and stirring.

Continue Cooking:
- Continue adding broth and stirring until the rice is creamy and cooked to al dente, usually around 18-20 minutes.

Sauté Sage:
- In a separate small pan, heat the remaining 1 tablespoon of butter. Add the chopped sage leaves and sauté until they become crispy. This will be used for garnish.

Finish with Parmesan:
- Remove the skillet from heat. Stir in the grated Parmesan cheese (if using). Mix until well combined.

Season and Serve:
- Season the risotto with salt and pepper to taste.

Garnish and Serve:
- Top the risotto with the crispy sage leaves and, if desired, roasted pumpkin seeds. Serve the Pumpkin and Sage Risotto warm.

Enjoy the warm and comforting flavors of fall with this pumpkin and sage risotto. It's a perfect dish for the autumn season and brings a touch of richness to your table.

Gorgonzola and Walnut Risotto

Ingredients:

- 1 1/2 cups Arborio rice
- 1/2 cup dry white wine
- 4 cups vegetable or chicken broth, kept warm
- 1 cup Gorgonzola cheese, crumbled
- 1/2 cup walnuts, chopped and toasted
- 1 small onion, finely chopped
- 2 cloves garlic, minced
- 2 tablespoons unsalted butter
- 2 tablespoons olive oil
- Salt and pepper, to taste
- Fresh parsley, chopped (for garnish)

Instructions:

Warm Broth:
- Heat the vegetable or chicken broth in a saucepan and keep it warm over low heat.

Sauté Onion and Garlic:
- In a large, heavy-bottomed skillet or pan, heat 1 tablespoon of butter and 1 tablespoon of olive oil over medium heat. Add the finely chopped onion and sauté until translucent. Add the minced garlic and cook for an additional 1-2 minutes.

Toast Rice:
- Add the Arborio rice to the pan and cook for about 2 minutes, stirring constantly, until the rice is lightly toasted.

Deglaze with Wine:
- Pour in the dry white wine, stirring continuously until the wine is mostly absorbed by the rice.

Begin Adding Broth:
- Start adding the warm vegetable or chicken broth, one ladle at a time, to the rice. Stir frequently and allow the liquid to be absorbed before adding more.

Incorporate Gorgonzola:

- When the rice is halfway cooked, stir in the crumbled Gorgonzola cheese. Continue adding broth and stirring.

Continue Cooking:
- Continue adding broth and stirring until the rice is creamy and cooked to al dente, usually around 18-20 minutes.

Fold in Toasted Walnuts:
- In the last few minutes of cooking, fold in the chopped and toasted walnuts.

Finish with Butter:
- Remove the skillet from heat. Stir in the remaining 1 tablespoon of butter. Mix until well combined.

Season and Serve:
- Season the risotto with salt and pepper to taste.

Garnish and Serve:
- Garnish with fresh chopped parsley. Serve the Gorgonzola and Walnut Risotto warm.

Enjoy the decadent combination of Gorgonzola and toasted walnuts in this creamy and savory risotto. It's a perfect dish for cheese lovers and those looking for a sophisticated and comforting meal.

Roasted Red Pepper Risotto

Ingredients:

- 1 1/2 cups Arborio rice
- 1/2 cup dry white wine
- 4 cups vegetable or chicken broth, kept warm
- 2 large red bell peppers
- 1 small onion, finely chopped
- 2 cloves garlic, minced
- 2 tablespoons olive oil
- 2 tablespoons unsalted butter
- 1/2 cup Parmesan cheese, grated (optional for a non-vegan version)
- Salt and pepper, to taste
- Fresh basil or parsley, chopped (for garnish)

Instructions:

Roast Red Peppers:
- Preheat your oven's broiler. Place the whole red peppers on a baking sheet and broil, turning occasionally, until the skin is charred and blistered. Remove from the oven and place the peppers in a bowl, covering it with plastic wrap. Let them cool, then peel off the skin, remove the seeds, and chop the roasted red peppers.

Warm Broth:
- Heat the vegetable or chicken broth in a saucepan and keep it warm over low heat.

Sauté Onion and Garlic:
- In a large, heavy-bottomed skillet or pan, heat 1 tablespoon of butter and 1 tablespoon of olive oil over medium heat. Add the finely chopped onion and sauté until translucent. Add the minced garlic and cook for an additional 1-2 minutes.

Toast Rice:
- Add the Arborio rice to the pan and cook for about 2 minutes, stirring constantly, until the rice is lightly toasted.

Deglaze with Wine:
- Pour in the dry white wine, stirring continuously until the wine is mostly absorbed by the rice.

Begin Adding Broth:

- Start adding the warm vegetable or chicken broth, one ladle at a time, to the rice. Stir frequently and allow the liquid to be absorbed before adding more.

Incorporate Roasted Red Peppers:
- When the rice is halfway cooked, stir in the chopped roasted red peppers. Continue adding broth and stirring.

Continue Cooking:
- Continue adding broth and stirring until the rice is creamy and cooked to al dente, usually around 18-20 minutes.

Finish with Butter and Parmesan:
- Remove the skillet from heat. Stir in the remaining 1 tablespoon of butter and the grated Parmesan cheese (if using). Mix until well combined.

Season and Serve:
- Season the risotto with salt and pepper to taste.

Garnish and Serve:
- Garnish with fresh chopped basil or parsley. Serve the Roasted Red Pepper Risotto warm.

Enjoy the smoky sweetness of roasted red peppers in this colorful and flavorful risotto. It's a perfect dish for adding a touch of sophistication to your dinner table.

Pesto Risotto

Ingredients:

- 1 1/2 cups Arborio rice
- 1/2 cup dry white wine
- 4 cups vegetable or chicken broth, kept warm
- 1 cup fresh basil leaves, packed
- 2 cloves garlic
- 1/3 cup pine nuts, toasted
- 1/2 cup Parmesan cheese, grated (plus extra for serving)
- 1/4 cup extra-virgin olive oil
- 1 small onion, finely chopped
- 2 tablespoons unsalted butter
- Salt and pepper, to taste
- Fresh basil, chopped (for garnish)

Instructions:

Make Pesto:
- In a food processor, combine the fresh basil, garlic, toasted pine nuts, Parmesan cheese, and olive oil. Blend until you have a smooth pesto sauce. Set aside.

Warm Broth:
- Heat the vegetable or chicken broth in a saucepan and keep it warm over low heat.

Sauté Onion:
- In a large, heavy-bottomed skillet or pan, heat 1 tablespoon of butter over medium heat. Add the finely chopped onion and sauté until translucent.

Toast Rice:
- Add the Arborio rice to the pan and cook for about 2 minutes, stirring constantly, until the rice is lightly toasted.

Deglaze with Wine:
- Pour in the dry white wine, stirring continuously until the wine is mostly absorbed by the rice.

Begin Adding Broth:
- Start adding the warm vegetable or chicken broth, one ladle at a time, to the rice. Stir frequently and allow the liquid to be absorbed before adding more.

Incorporate Pesto:
- When the rice is halfway cooked, stir in the prepared pesto sauce. Continue adding broth and stirring.

Continue Cooking:
- Continue adding broth and stirring until the rice is creamy and cooked to al dente, usually around 18-20 minutes.

Finish with Butter:
- Remove the skillet from heat. Stir in the remaining 1 tablespoon of butter. Mix until well combined.

Season and Serve:
- Season the risotto with salt and pepper to taste.

Garnish and Serve:
- Garnish with additional grated Parmesan cheese and chopped fresh basil. Serve the Pesto Risotto warm.

Enjoy the aromatic and flavorful pesto risotto, a perfect dish for pesto lovers and a delicious way to elevate classic risotto with the bright taste of basil.

Shrimp and Pea Risotto

Ingredients:

- 1 1/2 cups Arborio rice
- 1/2 cup dry white wine
- 4 cups seafood or vegetable broth, kept warm
- 1 pound (about 450g) shrimp, peeled and deveined
- 1 cup fresh or frozen peas
- 1 small onion, finely chopped
- 2 cloves garlic, minced
- 2 tablespoons olive oil
- 2 tablespoons unsalted butter
- 1/2 cup Parmesan cheese, grated (optional for a non-vegan version)
- Salt and pepper, to taste
- Fresh parsley, chopped (for garnish)
- Lemon wedges (for serving)

Instructions:

Warm Broth:
- Heat the seafood or vegetable broth in a saucepan and keep it warm over low heat.

Sauté Shrimp:
- In a large, heavy-bottomed skillet or pan, heat 1 tablespoon of olive oil over medium-high heat. Add the shrimp and cook until they turn pink and opaque, about 2-3 minutes per side. Remove the shrimp from the pan and set them aside.

Sauté Onion and Garlic:
- In the same pan, add another tablespoon of olive oil. Add the finely chopped onion and sauté until translucent. Add the minced garlic and cook for an additional 1-2 minutes.

Toast Rice:
- Add the Arborio rice to the pan and cook for about 2 minutes, stirring constantly, until the rice is lightly toasted.

Deglaze with Wine:
- Pour in the dry white wine, stirring continuously until the wine is mostly absorbed by the rice.

Begin Adding Broth:
- Start adding the warm seafood or vegetable broth, one ladle at a time, to the rice. Stir frequently and allow the liquid to be absorbed before adding more.

Incorporate Peas:
- When the rice is halfway cooked, add the fresh or frozen peas. Continue adding broth and stirring.

Continue Cooking:
- Continue adding broth and stirring until the rice is creamy and cooked to al dente, usually around 18-20 minutes.

Finish with Butter and Parmesan:
- Remove the skillet from heat. Stir in the remaining 1 tablespoon of butter and the grated Parmesan cheese (if using). Mix until well combined.

Season and Serve:
- Season the risotto with salt and pepper to taste.

Add Shrimp and Garnish:
- Fold in the cooked shrimp and allow them to heat through. Garnish with fresh chopped parsley.

Serve with Lemon Wedges:
- Serve the Shrimp and Pea Risotto warm, with lemon wedges on the side for squeezing over the dish.

Enjoy the delicious combination of shrimp and peas in this creamy and satisfying risotto. It's a perfect dish for seafood enthusiasts and makes for an elegant yet comforting meal.

Artichoke and Lemon Risotto

Ingredients:

- 1 1/2 cups Arborio rice
- 1/2 cup dry white wine
- 4 cups vegetable or chicken broth, kept warm
- 1 can (about 14 oz) artichoke hearts, drained and chopped
- Zest and juice of 1 lemon
- 1 small onion, finely chopped
- 2 cloves garlic, minced
- 2 tablespoons olive oil
- 2 tablespoons unsalted butter
- 1/2 cup Parmesan cheese, grated (optional for a non-vegan version)
- Salt and pepper, to taste
- Fresh parsley, chopped (for garnish)

Instructions:

Warm Broth:
- Heat the vegetable or chicken broth in a saucepan and keep it warm over low heat.

Sauté Onion and Garlic:
- In a large, heavy-bottomed skillet or pan, heat 1 tablespoon of butter and 1 tablespoon of olive oil over medium heat. Add the finely chopped onion and sauté until translucent. Add the minced garlic and cook for an additional 1-2 minutes.

Toast Rice:
- Add the Arborio rice to the pan and cook for about 2 minutes, stirring constantly, until the rice is lightly toasted.

Deglaze with Wine:
- Pour in the dry white wine, stirring continuously until the wine is mostly absorbed by the rice.

Begin Adding Broth:
- Start adding the warm vegetable or chicken broth, one ladle at a time, to the rice. Stir frequently and allow the liquid to be absorbed before adding more.

Incorporate Artichokes:

- When the rice is halfway cooked, stir in the chopped artichoke hearts. Continue adding broth and stirring.

Add Lemon Zest and Juice:
- Add the lemon zest and juice to the risotto. Continue adding broth and stirring until the rice is creamy and cooked to al dente, usually around 18-20 minutes.

Finish with Butter and Parmesan:
- Remove the skillet from heat. Stir in the remaining 1 tablespoon of butter and the grated Parmesan cheese (if using). Mix until well combined.

Season and Serve:
- Season the risotto with salt and pepper to taste.

Garnish and Serve:
- Garnish with fresh chopped parsley. Serve the Artichoke and Lemon Risotto warm.

Enjoy the vibrant and citrusy flavors of artichoke and lemon in this delightful risotto. It's a perfect dish for a light and refreshing meal, especially during the warmer seasons.

Tomato and Mozzarella Risotto

Ingredients:

- 1 1/2 cups Arborio rice
- 1/2 cup dry white wine
- 4 cups vegetable or chicken broth, kept warm
- 3 ripe tomatoes, diced
- 1 cup fresh mozzarella cheese, diced
- 1 small onion, finely chopped
- 2 cloves garlic, minced
- 2 tablespoons olive oil
- 2 tablespoons unsalted butter
- 1/2 cup Parmesan cheese, grated (optional for a non-vegan version)
- Salt and pepper, to taste
- Fresh basil, chopped (for garnish)

Instructions:

Warm Broth:
- Heat the vegetable or chicken broth in a saucepan and keep it warm over low heat.

Sauté Onion and Garlic:
- In a large, heavy-bottomed skillet or pan, heat 1 tablespoon of butter and 1 tablespoon of olive oil over medium heat. Add the finely chopped onion and sauté until translucent. Add the minced garlic and cook for an additional 1-2 minutes.

Toast Rice:
- Add the Arborio rice to the pan and cook for about 2 minutes, stirring constantly, until the rice is lightly toasted.

Deglaze with Wine:
- Pour in the dry white wine, stirring continuously until the wine is mostly absorbed by the rice.

Begin Adding Broth:
- Start adding the warm vegetable or chicken broth, one ladle at a time, to the rice. Stir frequently and allow the liquid to be absorbed before adding more.

Incorporate Tomatoes:

- When the rice is halfway cooked, stir in the diced tomatoes. Continue adding broth and stirring.

Continue Cooking:
- Continue adding broth and stirring until the rice is creamy and cooked to al dente, usually around 18-20 minutes.

Fold in Mozzarella:
- In the last few minutes of cooking, fold in the diced mozzarella cheese.

Finish with Butter and Parmesan:
- Remove the skillet from heat. Stir in the remaining 1 tablespoon of butter and the grated Parmesan cheese (if using). Mix until well combined.

Season and Serve:
- Season the risotto with salt and pepper to taste.

Garnish with Basil:
- Garnish with fresh chopped basil. Serve the Tomato and Mozzarella Risotto warm.

Enjoy the comforting and classic combination of tomatoes and mozzarella in this creamy and satisfying risotto. It's a perfect dish for showcasing the flavors of summer and is sure to be a crowd-pleaser.

Radicchio and Balsamic Risotto

Ingredients:

- 1 1/2 cups Arborio rice
- 1/2 cup dry white wine
- 4 cups vegetable or chicken broth, kept warm
- 1 small head of radicchio, finely chopped
- 2 tablespoons balsamic vinegar
- 1 small onion, finely chopped
- 2 cloves garlic, minced
- 2 tablespoons olive oil
- 2 tablespoons unsalted butter
- 1/2 cup Parmesan cheese, grated (optional for a non-vegan version)
- Salt and pepper, to taste
- Fresh parsley, chopped (for garnish)

Instructions:

Warm Broth:
- Heat the vegetable or chicken broth in a saucepan and keep it warm over low heat.

Sauté Onion and Garlic:
- In a large, heavy-bottomed skillet or pan, heat 1 tablespoon of butter and 1 tablespoon of olive oil over medium heat. Add the finely chopped onion and sauté until translucent. Add the minced garlic and cook for an additional 1-2 minutes.

Toast Rice:
- Add the Arborio rice to the pan and cook for about 2 minutes, stirring constantly, until the rice is lightly toasted.

Deglaze with Wine:
- Pour in the dry white wine, stirring continuously until the wine is mostly absorbed by the rice.

Begin Adding Broth:
- Start adding the warm vegetable or chicken broth, one ladle at a time, to the rice. Stir frequently and allow the liquid to be absorbed before adding more.

Incorporate Radicchio:

- When the rice is halfway cooked, stir in the finely chopped radicchio. Continue adding broth and stirring.

Add Balsamic Vinegar:
- Drizzle in the balsamic vinegar and continue adding broth until the rice is creamy and cooked to al dente, usually around 18-20 minutes.

Finish with Butter and Parmesan:
- Remove the skillet from heat. Stir in the remaining 1 tablespoon of butter and the grated Parmesan cheese (if using). Mix until well combined.

Season and Serve:
- Season the risotto with salt and pepper to taste.

Garnish with Parsley:
- Garnish with fresh chopped parsley. Serve the Radicchio and Balsamic Risotto warm.

Enjoy the unique and bold flavors of radicchio and balsamic vinegar in this risotto. It's a sophisticated and delicious dish that makes for a memorable meal.

Smoked Salmon Risotto

Ingredients:

- 1 1/2 cups Arborio rice
- 1/2 cup dry white wine
- 4 cups fish or vegetable broth, kept warm
- 200g smoked salmon, flaked
- 1 small onion, finely chopped
- 2 cloves garlic, minced
- 2 tablespoons olive oil
- 2 tablespoons unsalted butter
- 1/2 cup dry white wine
- 1/2 cup Parmesan cheese, grated
- Zest and juice of 1 lemon
- Salt and pepper, to taste
- Fresh dill, chopped (for garnish)

Instructions:

Warm Broth:
- Heat the fish or vegetable broth in a saucepan and keep it warm over low heat.

Sauté Onion and Garlic:
- In a large, heavy-bottomed skillet or pan, heat 1 tablespoon of butter and 1 tablespoon of olive oil over medium heat. Add the finely chopped onion and sauté until translucent. Add the minced garlic and cook for an additional 1-2 minutes.

Toast Rice:
- Add the Arborio rice to the pan and cook for about 2 minutes, stirring constantly, until the rice is lightly toasted.

Deglaze with Wine:
- Pour in the dry white wine, stirring continuously until the wine is mostly absorbed by the rice.

Begin Adding Broth:
- Start adding the warm fish or vegetable broth, one ladle at a time, to the rice. Stir frequently and allow the liquid to be absorbed before adding more.

Incorporate Smoked Salmon:
- When the rice is halfway cooked, stir in the flaked smoked salmon. Continue adding broth and stirring.

Add Lemon Zest and Juice:
- Zest the lemon and squeeze its juice into the risotto. Continue adding broth until the rice is creamy and cooked to al dente, usually around 18-20 minutes.

Finish with Butter and Parmesan:
- Remove the skillet from heat. Stir in the remaining 1 tablespoon of butter and the grated Parmesan cheese. Mix until well combined.

Season and Serve:
- Season the risotto with salt and pepper to taste.

Garnish with Dill:
- Garnish with fresh chopped dill. Serve the Smoked Salmon Risotto warm.

Enjoy the exquisite combination of creamy risotto and the smoky richness of salmon in this elegant and flavorful dish. It's perfect for a special occasion or to indulge in a gourmet meal at home.

Zucchini and Lemon Risotto

Ingredients:

- 1 1/2 cups Arborio rice
- 1/2 cup dry white wine
- 4 cups vegetable or chicken broth, kept warm
- 2 medium zucchinis, diced
- Zest and juice of 2 lemons
- 1 small onion, finely chopped
- 2 cloves garlic, minced
- 2 tablespoons olive oil
- 2 tablespoons unsalted butter
- 1/2 cup Parmesan cheese, grated (optional for a non-vegan version)
- Salt and pepper, to taste
- Fresh basil or parsley, chopped (for garnish)

Instructions:

Warm Broth:
- Heat the vegetable or chicken broth in a saucepan and keep it warm over low heat.

Sauté Onion and Garlic:
- In a large, heavy-bottomed skillet or pan, heat 1 tablespoon of butter and 1 tablespoon of olive oil over medium heat. Add the finely chopped onion and sauté until translucent. Add the minced garlic and cook for an additional 1-2 minutes.

Add Zucchini:
- Add the diced zucchini to the pan and sauté until it's just tender, about 3-4 minutes.

Toast Rice:
- Add the Arborio rice to the pan and cook for about 2 minutes, stirring constantly, until the rice is lightly toasted.

Deglaze with Wine:
- Pour in the dry white wine, stirring continuously until the wine is mostly absorbed by the rice.

Begin Adding Broth:

- Start adding the warm vegetable or chicken broth, one ladle at a time, to the rice. Stir frequently and allow the liquid to be absorbed before adding more.

Add Lemon Zest and Juice:
- Zest the lemons and squeeze their juice into the risotto. Continue adding broth until the rice is creamy and cooked to al dente, usually around 18-20 minutes.

Finish with Butter and Parmesan:
- Remove the skillet from heat. Stir in the remaining 1 tablespoon of butter and the grated Parmesan cheese (if using). Mix until well combined.

Season and Serve:
- Season the risotto with salt and pepper to taste.

Garnish with Basil or Parsley:
- Garnish with fresh chopped basil or parsley. Serve the Zucchini and Lemon Risotto warm.

Enjoy the light and summery flavors of zucchini and lemon in this vibrant risotto. It's a perfect dish for a fresh and satisfying meal, especially during the warmer seasons.

Porcini Mushroom Risotto

Ingredients:

- 1 1/2 cups Arborio rice
- 1/2 cup dry white wine
- 4 cups vegetable or chicken broth, kept warm
- 1 cup dried porcini mushrooms, rehydrated and chopped (reserve the soaking liquid)
- 1 cup fresh mushrooms (such as cremini or button), sliced
- 1 small onion, finely chopped
- 2 cloves garlic, minced
- 2 tablespoons olive oil
- 2 tablespoons unsalted butter
- 1/2 cup Parmesan cheese, grated (optional for a non-vegan version)
- Salt and pepper, to taste
- Fresh parsley, chopped (for garnish)

Instructions:

Rehydrate Porcini Mushrooms:
- Place the dried porcini mushrooms in a bowl and cover them with hot water. Let them soak for about 20-30 minutes until rehydrated. Strain the soaking liquid through a fine sieve or cheesecloth to remove any debris, and chop the rehydrated porcini mushrooms.

Warm Broth:
- Heat the vegetable or chicken broth in a saucepan and keep it warm over low heat. Add the strained porcini soaking liquid to the broth for added flavor.

Sauté Onion and Garlic:
- In a large, heavy-bottomed skillet or pan, heat 1 tablespoon of butter and 1 tablespoon of olive oil over medium heat. Add the finely chopped onion and sauté until translucent. Add the minced garlic and cook for an additional 1-2 minutes.

Add Fresh and Rehydrated Mushrooms:
- Add the sliced fresh mushrooms and the rehydrated porcini mushrooms to the pan. Sauté until the mushrooms are golden brown.

Toast Rice:

- Add the Arborio rice to the pan and cook for about 2 minutes, stirring constantly, until the rice is lightly toasted.

Deglaze with Wine:
- Pour in the dry white wine, stirring continuously until the wine is mostly absorbed by the rice.

Begin Adding Broth:
- Start adding the warm vegetable or chicken broth, one ladle at a time, to the rice. Stir frequently and allow the liquid to be absorbed before adding more.

Continue Cooking:
- Continue adding broth and stirring until the rice is creamy and cooked to al dente, usually around 18-20 minutes.

Finish with Butter and Parmesan:
- Remove the skillet from heat. Stir in the remaining 1 tablespoon of butter and the grated Parmesan cheese (if using). Mix until well combined.

Season and Serve:
- Season the risotto with salt and pepper to taste.

Garnish with Parsley:
- Garnish with fresh chopped parsley. Serve the Porcini Mushroom Risotto warm.

Enjoy the deep and savory flavor of porcini mushrooms in this creamy and satisfying risotto. It's a perfect dish for mushroom enthusiasts and adds a touch of elegance to your dining experience.

Roasted Vegetable Risotto

Ingredients:

- 1 1/2 cups Arborio rice
- 1/2 cup dry white wine
- 4 cups vegetable broth, kept warm
- Assorted vegetables for roasting (e.g., cherry tomatoes, bell peppers, zucchini, carrots, mushrooms)
- 1 small onion, finely chopped
- 2 cloves garlic, minced
- 2 tablespoons olive oil
- 2 tablespoons unsalted butter
- 1/2 cup Parmesan cheese, grated (optional for a non-vegan version)
- Salt and pepper, to taste
- Fresh herbs (e.g., thyme, rosemary, parsley), chopped (for garnish)

Instructions:

Preheat Oven:
- Preheat your oven to 400°F (200°C).

Roast Vegetables:
- Cut the assorted vegetables into bite-sized pieces. Place them on a baking sheet, drizzle with olive oil, and season with salt and pepper. Roast in the preheated oven until the vegetables are tender and slightly caramelized, about 20-25 minutes.

Warm Broth:
- Heat the vegetable broth in a saucepan and keep it warm over low heat.

Sauté Onion and Garlic:
- In a large, heavy-bottomed skillet or pan, heat 1 tablespoon of butter and 1 tablespoon of olive oil over medium heat. Add the finely chopped onion and sauté until translucent. Add the minced garlic and cook for an additional 1-2 minutes.

Toast Rice:
- Add the Arborio rice to the pan and cook for about 2 minutes, stirring constantly, until the rice is lightly toasted.

Deglaze with Wine:
- Pour in the dry white wine, stirring continuously until the wine is mostly absorbed by the rice.

Begin Adding Broth:
- Start adding the warm vegetable broth, one ladle at a time, to the rice. Stir frequently and allow the liquid to be absorbed before adding more.

Incorporate Roasted Vegetables:
- When the rice is halfway cooked, fold in the roasted vegetables. Continue adding broth and stirring.

Continue Cooking:
- Continue adding broth and stirring until the rice is creamy and cooked to al dente, usually around 18-20 minutes.

Finish with Butter and Parmesan:
- Remove the skillet from heat. Stir in the remaining 1 tablespoon of butter and the grated Parmesan cheese (if using). Mix until well combined.

Season and Serve:
- Season the risotto with salt and pepper to taste.

Garnish with Fresh Herbs:
- Garnish with chopped fresh herbs. Serve the Roasted Vegetable Risotto warm.

Enjoy the medley of flavors and textures in this hearty and satisfying roasted vegetable risotto. It's a versatile dish that you can customize based on your favorite vegetables and herbs.

Sun-Dried Tomato Risotto

Ingredients:

- 1 1/2 cups Arborio rice
- 1/2 cup dry white wine
- 4 cups vegetable or chicken broth, kept warm
- 1 cup sun-dried tomatoes (packed in oil), drained and chopped
- 1 small onion, finely chopped
- 2 cloves garlic, minced
- 2 tablespoons olive oil (from the sun-dried tomatoes jar, if available)
- 2 tablespoons unsalted butter
- 1/2 cup Parmesan cheese, grated (optional for a non-vegan version)
- Salt and pepper, to taste
- Fresh basil, chopped (for garnish)

Instructions:

Warm Broth:
- Heat the vegetable or chicken broth in a saucepan and keep it warm over low heat.

Sauté Onion and Garlic:
- In a large, heavy-bottomed skillet or pan, heat 1 tablespoon of butter and 1 tablespoon of olive oil (you can use oil from the sun-dried tomatoes jar for added flavor) over medium heat. Add the finely chopped onion and sauté until translucent. Add the minced garlic and cook for an additional 1-2 minutes.

Add Sun-Dried Tomatoes:
- Add the chopped sun-dried tomatoes to the pan. Sauté for a few minutes to release their flavors.

Toast Rice:
- Add the Arborio rice to the pan and cook for about 2 minutes, stirring constantly, until the rice is lightly toasted.

Deglaze with Wine:
- Pour in the dry white wine, stirring continuously until the wine is mostly absorbed by the rice.

Begin Adding Broth:

- Start adding the warm vegetable or chicken broth, one ladle at a time, to the rice. Stir frequently and allow the liquid to be absorbed before adding more.

Continue Cooking:
- Continue adding broth and stirring until the rice is creamy and cooked to al dente, usually around 18-20 minutes.

Finish with Butter and Parmesan:
- Remove the skillet from heat. Stir in the remaining 1 tablespoon of butter and the grated Parmesan cheese (if using). Mix until well combined.

Season and Serve:
- Season the risotto with salt and pepper to taste.

Garnish with Fresh Basil:
- Garnish with chopped fresh basil. Serve the Sun-Dried Tomato Risotto warm.

Enjoy the rich and savory flavor of sun-dried tomatoes in this creamy and comforting risotto. It's a delightful dish that brings a burst of Mediterranean flavors to your table.

Lobster Risotto

Ingredients:

- 1 1/2 cups Arborio rice
- 1/2 cup dry white wine
- 4 cups seafood or chicken broth, kept warm
- 2 lobster tails, shells removed and meat chopped into bite-sized pieces
- 1 small onion, finely chopped
- 2 cloves garlic, minced
- 2 tablespoons olive oil
- 2 tablespoons unsalted butter
- 1/2 cup Parmesan cheese, grated
- Zest and juice of 1 lemon
- Salt and pepper, to taste
- Fresh parsley, chopped (for garnish)

Instructions:

Prepare Lobster:
- Remove the shells from the lobster tails and chop the meat into bite-sized pieces.

Warm Broth:
- Heat the seafood or chicken broth in a saucepan and keep it warm over low heat.

Sauté Onion and Garlic:
- In a large, heavy-bottomed skillet or pan, heat 1 tablespoon of butter and 1 tablespoon of olive oil over medium heat. Add the finely chopped onion and sauté until translucent. Add the minced garlic and cook for an additional 1-2 minutes.

Cook Lobster:
- Add the chopped lobster meat to the pan and sauté until it turns opaque, about 3-4 minutes. Remove the lobster from the pan and set it aside.

Toast Rice:
- Add the Arborio rice to the pan and cook for about 2 minutes, stirring constantly, until the rice is lightly toasted.

Deglaze with Wine:
- Pour in the dry white wine, stirring continuously until the wine is mostly absorbed by the rice.

Begin Adding Broth:
- Start adding the warm seafood or chicken broth, one ladle at a time, to the rice. Stir frequently and allow the liquid to be absorbed before adding more.

Continue Cooking:
- Continue adding broth and stirring until the rice is creamy and cooked to al dente, usually around 18-20 minutes.

Finish with Butter and Parmesan:
- Remove the skillet from heat. Stir in the remaining 1 tablespoon of butter and the grated Parmesan cheese. Mix until well combined.

Fold in Lobster and Add Lemon:
- Fold in the cooked lobster pieces and add the lemon zest and juice. Mix gently to combine.

Season and Serve:
- Season the risotto with salt and pepper to taste.

Garnish with Parsley:
- Garnish with chopped fresh parsley. Serve the Lobster Risotto warm.

Enjoy the exquisite taste of lobster in this creamy and decadent risotto. It's a perfect dish for special occasions or when you want to treat yourself to an elegant and delightful meal.

Spring Vegetable Risotto

Ingredients:

- 1 1/2 cups Arborio rice
- 1/2 cup dry white wine
- 4 cups vegetable broth, kept warm
- 1 cup asparagus, trimmed and cut into bite-sized pieces
- 1 cup peas (fresh or frozen)
- 1 small zucchini, diced
- 1 small yellow squash, diced
- 1 small onion, finely chopped
- 2 cloves garlic, minced
- 2 tablespoons olive oil
- 2 tablespoons unsalted butter
- 1/2 cup Parmesan cheese, grated (optional for a non-vegan version)
- Zest and juice of 1 lemon
- Salt and pepper, to taste
- Fresh herbs (e.g., basil, chives, mint), chopped (for garnish)

Instructions:

Warm Broth:
- Heat the vegetable broth in a saucepan and keep it warm over low heat.

Sauté Onion and Garlic:
- In a large, heavy-bottomed skillet or pan, heat 1 tablespoon of butter and 1 tablespoon of olive oil over medium heat. Add the finely chopped onion and sauté until translucent. Add the minced garlic and cook for an additional 1-2 minutes.

Add Asparagus, Peas, Zucchini, and Yellow Squash:
- Add the asparagus, peas, diced zucchini, and diced yellow squash to the pan. Sauté for a few minutes until the vegetables are slightly tender.

Toast Rice:
- Add the Arborio rice to the pan and cook for about 2 minutes, stirring constantly, until the rice is lightly toasted.

Deglaze with Wine:
- Pour in the dry white wine, stirring continuously until the wine is mostly absorbed by the rice.

Begin Adding Broth:
- Start adding the warm vegetable broth, one ladle at a time, to the rice. Stir frequently and allow the liquid to be absorbed before adding more.

Continue Cooking:
- Continue adding broth and stirring until the rice is creamy and cooked to al dente, usually around 18-20 minutes.

Finish with Butter and Parmesan:
- Remove the skillet from heat. Stir in the remaining 1 tablespoon of butter and the grated Parmesan cheese (if using). Mix until well combined.

Add Lemon Zest and Juice:
- Add the lemon zest and juice to the risotto. Mix gently to incorporate the citrusy flavors.

Season and Serve:
- Season the risotto with salt and pepper to taste.

Garnish with Fresh Herbs:
- Garnish with chopped fresh herbs of your choice, such as basil, chives, or mint. Serve the Spring Vegetable Risotto warm.

Enjoy the burst of flavors and colors in this delightful spring vegetable risotto. It's a perfect dish to celebrate the season's produce and create a light and satisfying meal.

Ricotta and Spinach Risotto

Ingredients:

- 1 1/2 cups Arborio rice
- 1/2 cup dry white wine
- 4 cups vegetable broth, kept warm
- 1 cup fresh spinach, chopped
- 1 cup ricotta cheese
- 1 small onion, finely chopped
- 2 cloves garlic, minced
- 2 tablespoons olive oil
- 2 tablespoons unsalted butter
- 1/2 cup Parmesan cheese, grated (optional for a non-vegan version)
- Salt and pepper, to taste
- Fresh basil or parsley, chopped (for garnish)

Instructions:

Warm Broth:
- Heat the vegetable broth in a saucepan and keep it warm over low heat.

Sauté Onion and Garlic:
- In a large, heavy-bottomed skillet or pan, heat 1 tablespoon of butter and 1 tablespoon of olive oil over medium heat. Add the finely chopped onion and sauté until translucent. Add the minced garlic and cook for an additional 1-2 minutes.

Add Spinach:
- Add the chopped fresh spinach to the pan and sauté until wilted.

Toast Rice:
- Add the Arborio rice to the pan and cook for about 2 minutes, stirring constantly, until the rice is lightly toasted.

Deglaze with Wine:
- Pour in the dry white wine, stirring continuously until the wine is mostly absorbed by the rice.

Begin Adding Broth:
- Start adding the warm vegetable broth, one ladle at a time, to the rice. Stir frequently and allow the liquid to be absorbed before adding more.

Continue Cooking:

- Continue adding broth and stirring until the rice is creamy and cooked to al dente, usually around 18-20 minutes.

Add Ricotta:
- Stir in the ricotta cheese, mixing well to incorporate its creaminess into the risotto.

Finish with Butter and Parmesan:
- Remove the skillet from heat. Stir in the remaining 1 tablespoon of butter and the grated Parmesan cheese (if using). Mix until well combined.

Season and Serve:
- Season the risotto with salt and pepper to taste.

Garnish with Fresh Basil or Parsley:
- Garnish with chopped fresh basil or parsley. Serve the Ricotta and Spinach Risotto warm.

Enjoy the luscious combination of creamy ricotta and vibrant spinach in this comforting and satisfying risotto. It's a perfect dish for a comforting meal or to impress guests with its rich flavors.

Beetroot and Goat Cheese Risotto

Ingredients:

- 1 1/2 cups Arborio rice
- 1/2 cup dry white wine
- 4 cups vegetable broth, kept warm
- 2 medium-sized beetroots, roasted, peeled, and grated
- 4 ounces (about 113g) goat cheese, crumbled
- 1 small onion, finely chopped
- 2 cloves garlic, minced
- 2 tablespoons olive oil
- 2 tablespoons unsalted butter
- 1/2 cup Parmesan cheese, grated (optional for a non-vegan version)
- Salt and pepper, to taste
- Fresh thyme or basil, chopped (for garnish)

Instructions:

Roast and Prepare Beetroots:
- Preheat your oven to 400°F (200°C). Wrap the beetroots in foil and roast them until they are tender when pierced with a fork, usually about 45-60 minutes. Once cooled, peel and grate the beetroots.

Warm Broth:
- Heat the vegetable broth in a saucepan and keep it warm over low heat.

Sauté Onion and Garlic:
- In a large, heavy-bottomed skillet or pan, heat 1 tablespoon of butter and 1 tablespoon of olive oil over medium heat. Add the finely chopped onion and sauté until translucent. Add the minced garlic and cook for an additional 1-2 minutes.

Add Grated Beetroots:
- Add the grated roasted beetroots to the pan. Sauté for a few minutes to infuse their flavor into the risotto.

Toast Rice:
- Add the Arborio rice to the pan and cook for about 2 minutes, stirring constantly, until the rice is lightly toasted.

Deglaze with Wine:
- Pour in the dry white wine, stirring continuously until the wine is mostly absorbed by the rice.

Begin Adding Broth:
- Start adding the warm vegetable broth, one ladle at a time, to the rice. Stir frequently and allow the liquid to be absorbed before adding more.

Continue Cooking:
- Continue adding broth and stirring until the rice is creamy and cooked to al dente, usually around 18-20 minutes.

Fold in Goat Cheese:
- Once the rice is cooked, fold in the crumbled goat cheese. Mix gently until the goat cheese is melted and incorporated into the risotto.

Finish with Butter and Parmesan:
- Remove the skillet from heat. Stir in the remaining 1 tablespoon of butter and the grated Parmesan cheese (if using). Mix until well combined.

Season and Serve:
- Season the risotto with salt and pepper to taste.

Garnish with Fresh Thyme or Basil:
- Garnish with chopped fresh thyme or basil. Serve the Beetroot and Goat Cheese Risotto warm.

Enjoy the vibrant colors and delightful combination of flavors in this unique beetroot and goat cheese risotto. It's a visually stunning dish that's perfect for both casual dinners and special occasions.

Lemon and Mint Risotto

Ingredients:

- 1 1/2 cups Arborio rice
- 1/2 cup dry white wine
- 4 cups vegetable or chicken broth, kept warm
- Zest and juice of 2 lemons
- 1/4 cup fresh mint leaves, finely chopped
- 1 small onion, finely chopped
- 2 cloves garlic, minced
- 2 tablespoons olive oil
- 2 tablespoons unsalted butter
- 1/2 cup Parmesan cheese, grated (optional for a non-vegan version)
- Salt and pepper, to taste

Instructions:

Warm Broth:
- Heat the vegetable or chicken broth in a saucepan and keep it warm over low heat.

Sauté Onion and Garlic:
- In a large, heavy-bottomed skillet or pan, heat 1 tablespoon of butter and 1 tablespoon of olive oil over medium heat. Add the finely chopped onion and sauté until translucent. Add the minced garlic and cook for an additional 1-2 minutes.

Add Lemon Zest:
- Add the zest of 2 lemons to the pan, stirring to infuse the risotto with citrusy flavors.

Toast Rice:
- Add the Arborio rice to the pan and cook for about 2 minutes, stirring constantly, until the rice is lightly toasted.

Deglaze with Wine:
- Pour in the dry white wine, stirring continuously until the wine is mostly absorbed by the rice.

Begin Adding Broth:
- Start adding the warm vegetable or chicken broth, one ladle at a time, to the rice. Stir frequently and allow the liquid to be absorbed before adding more.

Continue Cooking:
- Continue adding broth and stirring until the rice is creamy and cooked to al dente, usually around 18-20 minutes.

Fold in Lemon Juice and Mint:
- Squeeze the juice of 2 lemons into the risotto and fold in the finely chopped mint leaves. Mix gently to incorporate the citrusy and minty flavors.

Finish with Butter and Parmesan:
- Remove the skillet from heat. Stir in the remaining 1 tablespoon of butter and the grated Parmesan cheese (if using). Mix until well combined.

Season and Serve:
- Season the risotto with salt and pepper to taste.

Garnish with Extra Mint:
- Garnish the Lemon and Mint Risotto with extra chopped mint leaves. Serve it warm.

Enjoy the light and refreshing taste of lemon and mint in this vibrant risotto. It's a perfect dish for a spring or summer meal, bringing a burst of citrusy and herbal goodness to your table.

Caramelized Onion and Gouda Risotto

Ingredients:

- 1 1/2 cups Arborio rice
- 1/2 cup dry white wine
- 4 cups vegetable or chicken broth, kept warm
- 2 large onions, thinly sliced
- 1 cup Gouda cheese, shredded
- 1 small garlic clove, minced
- 2 tablespoons olive oil
- 2 tablespoons unsalted butter
- 1/2 cup Parmesan cheese, grated (optional for a non-vegan version)
- Salt and pepper, to taste
- Fresh thyme or parsley, chopped (for garnish)

Instructions:

Caramelize Onions:
- In a large skillet, heat 1 tablespoon of olive oil over medium-low heat. Add the thinly sliced onions and cook, stirring occasionally, until they become soft and caramelized, about 20-30 minutes. If needed, add a splash of water to deglaze the pan and prevent burning.

Warm Broth:
- Heat the vegetable or chicken broth in a saucepan and keep it warm over low heat.

Sauté Garlic:
- In a separate large, heavy-bottomed skillet or pan, heat the remaining 1 tablespoon of olive oil and 1 tablespoon of butter over medium heat. Add the minced garlic and sauté for about 1-2 minutes until fragrant.

Add Rice:
- Add the Arborio rice to the pan and cook for about 2 minutes, stirring constantly, until the rice is lightly toasted.

Deglaze with Wine:
- Pour in the dry white wine, stirring continuously until the wine is mostly absorbed by the rice.

Begin Adding Broth:

- Start adding the warm vegetable or chicken broth, one ladle at a time, to the rice. Stir frequently and allow the liquid to be absorbed before adding more.

Continue Cooking:
- Continue adding broth and stirring until the rice is creamy and cooked to al dente, usually around 18-20 minutes.

Fold in Caramelized Onions and Gouda:
- Once the rice is almost cooked, fold in the caramelized onions and shredded Gouda cheese. Mix gently until the cheese is melted and the onions are evenly distributed.

Finish with Butter and Parmesan:
- Remove the skillet from heat. Stir in the remaining 1 tablespoon of butter and the grated Parmesan cheese (if using). Mix until well combined.

Season and Serve:
- Season the risotto with salt and pepper to taste.

Garnish with Fresh Herbs:
- Garnish with chopped fresh thyme or parsley. Serve the Caramelized Onion and Gouda Risotto warm.

Enjoy the luxurious and comforting combination of caramelized onions and Gouda cheese in this delicious risotto. It's a perfect dish for showcasing rich flavors and making any meal feel special.

Broccoli and Cheddar Risotto

Ingredients:

- 1 1/2 cups Arborio rice
- 1/2 cup dry white wine
- 4 cups vegetable or chicken broth, kept warm
- 2 cups broccoli florets, blanched
- 1 1/2 cups sharp cheddar cheese, shredded
- 1 small onion, finely chopped
- 2 cloves garlic, minced
- 2 tablespoons olive oil
- 2 tablespoons unsalted butter
- 1/2 cup Parmesan cheese, grated (optional for a non-vegan version)
- Salt and pepper, to taste
- Fresh parsley, chopped (for garnish)

Instructions:

Blanch Broccoli:
- Bring a pot of salted water to a boil. Add the broccoli florets and cook for 2-3 minutes until they are bright green and slightly tender. Drain and immediately transfer the broccoli to a bowl of ice water to stop the cooking process. Set aside.

Warm Broth:
- Heat the vegetable or chicken broth in a saucepan and keep it warm over low heat.

Sauté Onion and Garlic:
- In a large, heavy-bottomed skillet or pan, heat 1 tablespoon of butter and 1 tablespoon of olive oil over medium heat. Add the finely chopped onion and sauté until translucent. Add the minced garlic and cook for an additional 1-2 minutes.

Add Rice:
- Add the Arborio rice to the pan and cook for about 2 minutes, stirring constantly, until the rice is lightly toasted.

Deglaze with Wine:
- Pour in the dry white wine, stirring continuously until the wine is mostly absorbed by the rice.

Begin Adding Broth:
- Start adding the warm vegetable or chicken broth, one ladle at a time, to the rice. Stir frequently and allow the liquid to be absorbed before adding more.

Continue Cooking:
- Continue adding broth and stirring until the rice is creamy and cooked to al dente, usually around 18-20 minutes.

Fold in Broccoli and Cheddar:
- Once the rice is almost cooked, fold in the blanched broccoli and shredded cheddar cheese. Mix gently until the cheese is melted and the broccoli is evenly distributed.

Finish with Butter and Parmesan:
- Remove the skillet from heat. Stir in the remaining 1 tablespoon of butter and the grated Parmesan cheese (if using). Mix until well combined.

Season and Serve:
- Season the risotto with salt and pepper to taste.

Garnish with Fresh Parsley:
- Garnish with chopped fresh parsley. Serve the Broccoli and Cheddar Risotto warm.

Enjoy the comforting combination of broccoli and cheddar cheese in this creamy and satisfying risotto. It's a perfect dish for a cozy and flavorful meal.

Brown Butter and Sage Risotto

Ingredients:

- 1 1/2 cups Arborio rice
- 1/2 cup dry white wine
- 4 cups vegetable or chicken broth, kept warm
- 1/2 cup unsalted butter
- 1/4 cup fresh sage leaves, chopped
- 1 small onion, finely chopped
- 2 cloves garlic, minced
- Salt and pepper, to taste
- 1/2 cup Parmesan cheese, grated (optional for a non-vegan version)

Instructions:

Warm Broth:
- Heat the vegetable or chicken broth in a saucepan and keep it warm over low heat.

Brown Butter and Sage:
- In a separate skillet, melt the butter over medium heat. Once melted, add the chopped sage leaves. Allow the butter to continue cooking, stirring frequently, until it turns golden brown and develops a nutty aroma. Be careful not to burn the butter. Once browned, remove from heat and set aside.

Sauté Onion and Garlic:
- In a large, heavy-bottomed skillet or pan, heat a small amount of the browned sage butter over medium heat. Add the finely chopped onion and sauté until translucent. Add the minced garlic and cook for an additional 1-2 minutes.

Add Rice:
- Add the Arborio rice to the pan and cook for about 2 minutes, stirring constantly, until the rice is lightly toasted.

Deglaze with Wine:
- Pour in the dry white wine, stirring continuously until the wine is mostly absorbed by the rice.

Begin Adding Broth:

- Start adding the warm vegetable or chicken broth, one ladle at a time, to the rice. Stir frequently and allow the liquid to be absorbed before adding more.

Continue Cooking:
- Continue adding broth and stirring until the rice is creamy and cooked to al dente, usually around 18-20 minutes.

Finish with Brown Butter and Sage:
- When the rice is almost cooked, fold in the remaining browned butter and sage mixture. Mix gently until well incorporated.

Season and Serve:
- Season the risotto with salt and pepper to taste.

Optional Parmesan Addition:
- If desired, stir in the grated Parmesan cheese to add extra creaminess to the risotto.

Serve Warm:
- Serve the Brown Butter and Sage Risotto warm, garnished with additional fresh sage leaves if desired.

Enjoy the rich and nutty flavor of brown butter paired with the aromatic essence of sage in this delightful risotto. It's a comforting dish that's perfect for showcasing the simple yet exquisite combination of these two ingredients.

Burrata and Cherry Tomato Risotto

Ingredients:

- 1 1/2 cups Arborio rice
- 1/2 cup dry white wine
- 4 cups vegetable or chicken broth, kept warm
- 1 cup cherry tomatoes, halved
- 1 ball of burrata cheese
- 1 small onion, finely chopped
- 2 cloves garlic, minced
- 2 tablespoons olive oil
- 2 tablespoons unsalted butter
- Salt and pepper, to taste
- Fresh basil, chopped (for garnish)

Instructions:

Warm Broth:
- Heat the vegetable or chicken broth in a saucepan and keep it warm over low heat.

Sauté Onion and Garlic:
- In a large, heavy-bottomed skillet or pan, heat 1 tablespoon of butter and 1 tablespoon of olive oil over medium heat. Add the finely chopped onion and sauté until translucent. Add the minced garlic and cook for an additional 1-2 minutes.

Add Rice:
- Add the Arborio rice to the pan and cook for about 2 minutes, stirring constantly, until the rice is lightly toasted.

Deglaze with Wine:
- Pour in the dry white wine, stirring continuously until the wine is mostly absorbed by the rice.

Begin Adding Broth:
- Start adding the warm vegetable or chicken broth, one ladle at a time, to the rice. Stir frequently and allow the liquid to be absorbed before adding more.

Continue Cooking:

- Continue adding broth and stirring until the rice is creamy and cooked to al dente, usually around 18-20 minutes.

Fold in Cherry Tomatoes:
- Once the rice is almost cooked, fold in the halved cherry tomatoes. Mix gently to incorporate the tomatoes into the risotto.

Finish with Butter:
- Remove the skillet from heat. Stir in the remaining 1 tablespoon of butter. Mix until well combined.

Season and Serve:
- Season the risotto with salt and pepper to taste.

Serve with Burrata:
- Place a generous spoonful of the creamy burrata cheese on top of each serving of risotto.

Garnish with Fresh Basil:
- Garnish with chopped fresh basil. Serve the Burrata and Cherry Tomato Risotto warm.

Enjoy the luxurious combination of creamy burrata and sweet cherry tomatoes in this delicious risotto. It's a perfect dish for celebrating the flavors of summer and indulging in a comforting and satisfying meal.

Eggplant and Tomato Risotto

Ingredients:

- 1 1/2 cups Arborio rice
- 1/2 cup dry white wine
- 4 cups vegetable or chicken broth, kept warm
- 1 medium-sized eggplant, diced
- 1 cup cherry tomatoes, halved
- 1 can (14 oz) diced tomatoes (with juices)
- 1 small onion, finely chopped
- 2 cloves garlic, minced
- 2 tablespoons olive oil
- 2 tablespoons unsalted butter
- 1/2 cup Parmesan cheese, grated (optional for a non-vegan version)
- Salt and pepper, to taste
- Fresh basil, chopped (for garnish)

Instructions:

Warm Broth:
- Heat the vegetable or chicken broth in a saucepan and keep it warm over low heat.

Sauté Onion and Garlic:
- In a large, heavy-bottomed skillet or pan, heat 1 tablespoon of butter and 1 tablespoon of olive oil over medium heat. Add the finely chopped onion and sauté until translucent. Add the minced garlic and cook for an additional 1-2 minutes.

Add Eggplant:
- Add the diced eggplant to the pan. Sauté until the eggplant is golden brown and softened.

Add Rice:
- Add the Arborio rice to the pan and cook for about 2 minutes, stirring constantly, until the rice is lightly toasted.

Deglaze with Wine:
- Pour in the dry white wine, stirring continuously until the wine is mostly absorbed by the rice.

Begin Adding Broth:

- Start adding the warm vegetable or chicken broth, one ladle at a time, to the rice. Stir frequently and allow the liquid to be absorbed before adding more.

Add Canned and Cherry Tomatoes:
- Once the rice is partially cooked, add the diced canned tomatoes (with juices) and the halved cherry tomatoes to the pan. Continue adding broth and stirring.

Continue Cooking:
- Continue adding broth and stirring until the rice is creamy and cooked to al dente, usually around 18-20 minutes.

Finish with Butter and Parmesan:
- Remove the skillet from heat. Stir in the remaining 1 tablespoon of butter and the grated Parmesan cheese (if using). Mix until well combined.

Season and Serve:
- Season the risotto with salt and pepper to taste.

Garnish with Fresh Basil:
- Garnish with chopped fresh basil. Serve the Eggplant and Tomato Risotto warm.

Enjoy the hearty combination of eggplant and tomatoes in this flavorful risotto. It's a perfect dish for showcasing the bountiful flavors of summer and creating a comforting and delicious meal.

Pomegranate and Feta Risotto

Ingredients:

- 1 1/2 cups Arborio rice
- 1/2 cup dry white wine
- 4 cups vegetable or chicken broth, kept warm
- 1 cup pomegranate arils (seeds)
- 1/2 cup crumbled feta cheese
- 1 small onion, finely chopped
- 2 cloves garlic, minced
- 2 tablespoons olive oil
- 2 tablespoons unsalted butter
- 1/2 cup Parmesan cheese, grated (optional for a non-vegan version)
- Salt and pepper, to taste
- Fresh parsley, chopped (for garnish)

Instructions:

Warm Broth:
- Heat the vegetable or chicken broth in a saucepan and keep it warm over low heat.

Sauté Onion and Garlic:
- In a large, heavy-bottomed skillet or pan, heat 1 tablespoon of butter and 1 tablespoon of olive oil over medium heat. Add the finely chopped onion and sauté until translucent. Add the minced garlic and cook for an additional 1-2 minutes.

Add Rice:
- Add the Arborio rice to the pan and cook for about 2 minutes, stirring constantly, until the rice is lightly toasted.

Deglaze with Wine:
- Pour in the dry white wine, stirring continuously until the wine is mostly absorbed by the rice.

Begin Adding Broth:
- Start adding the warm vegetable or chicken broth, one ladle at a time, to the rice. Stir frequently and allow the liquid to be absorbed before adding more.

Continue Cooking:

- Continue adding broth and stirring until the rice is creamy and cooked to al dente, usually around 18-20 minutes.

Fold in Pomegranate Arils and Feta:
- Once the rice is almost cooked, fold in the pomegranate arils and crumbled feta cheese. Mix gently until the feta is slightly melted and the pomegranate arils are evenly distributed.

Finish with Butter and Parmesan:
- Remove the skillet from heat. Stir in the remaining 1 tablespoon of butter and the grated Parmesan cheese (if using). Mix until well combined.

Season and Serve:
- Season the risotto with salt and pepper to taste.

Garnish with Fresh Parsley:
- Garnish with chopped fresh parsley. Serve the Pomegranate and Feta Risotto warm.

Enjoy the delightful combination of sweet pomegranate arils and tangy feta cheese in this colorful and flavorful risotto. It's a unique dish that's sure to impress with its vibrant taste and eye-catching presentation.

Green Pea and Pancetta Risotto

Ingredients:

- 1 1/2 cups Arborio rice
- 1/2 cup dry white wine
- 4 cups chicken or vegetable broth, kept warm
- 1 cup frozen green peas, thawed
- 1/2 cup pancetta, diced
- 1 small onion, finely chopped
- 2 cloves garlic, minced
- 2 tablespoons olive oil
- 2 tablespoons unsalted butter
- 1/2 cup Parmesan cheese, grated (optional for a non-vegan version)
- Salt and pepper, to taste
- Fresh mint or parsley, chopped (for garnish)

Instructions:

Warm Broth:
- Heat the chicken or vegetable broth in a saucepan and keep it warm over low heat.

Sauté Onion and Garlic:
- In a large, heavy-bottomed skillet or pan, heat 1 tablespoon of butter and 1 tablespoon of olive oil over medium heat. Add the finely chopped onion and sauté until translucent. Add the minced garlic and cook for an additional 1-2 minutes.

Add Pancetta:
- Add the diced pancetta to the pan. Sauté until the pancetta is golden and crispy.

Add Rice:
- Add the Arborio rice to the pan and cook for about 2 minutes, stirring constantly, until the rice is lightly toasted.

Deglaze with Wine:
- Pour in the dry white wine, stirring continuously until the wine is mostly absorbed by the rice.

Begin Adding Broth:

- Start adding the warm chicken or vegetable broth, one ladle at a time, to the rice. Stir frequently and allow the liquid to be absorbed before adding more.

Continue Cooking:
- Continue adding broth and stirring until the rice is creamy and cooked to al dente, usually around 18-20 minutes.

Fold in Green Peas:
- Once the rice is almost cooked, fold in the thawed green peas. Mix gently to incorporate the peas into the risotto.

Finish with Butter and Parmesan:
- Remove the skillet from heat. Stir in the remaining 1 tablespoon of butter and the grated Parmesan cheese (if using). Mix until well combined.

Season and Serve:
- Season the risotto with salt and pepper to taste.

Garnish with Fresh Mint or Parsley:
- Garnish with chopped fresh mint or parsley. Serve the Green Pea and Pancetta Risotto warm.

Enjoy the burst of freshness from green peas and the savory crunch of pancetta in this flavorful risotto. It's a delicious and comforting dish that's perfect for a cozy dinner.

Wild Mushroom Risotto

Ingredients:

- 1 1/2 cups Arborio rice
- 1/2 cup dry white wine
- 4 cups vegetable or chicken broth, kept warm
- 1 cup mixed wild mushrooms (such as shiitake, oyster, and cremini), cleaned and sliced
- 1 small onion, finely chopped
- 2 cloves garlic, minced
- 2 tablespoons olive oil
- 2 tablespoons unsalted butter
- 1/2 cup Parmesan cheese, grated (optional for a non-vegan version)
- Salt and pepper, to taste
- Fresh parsley, chopped (for garnish)

Instructions:

Warm Broth:
- Heat the vegetable or chicken broth in a saucepan and keep it warm over low heat.

Sauté Onion and Garlic:
- In a large, heavy-bottomed skillet or pan, heat 1 tablespoon of butter and 1 tablespoon of olive oil over medium heat. Add the finely chopped onion and sauté until translucent. Add the minced garlic and cook for an additional 1-2 minutes.

Add Wild Mushrooms:
- Add the sliced wild mushrooms to the pan. Sauté until the mushrooms are golden brown and any liquid released has evaporated.

Add Rice:
- Add the Arborio rice to the pan and cook for about 2 minutes, stirring constantly, until the rice is lightly toasted.

Deglaze with Wine:
- Pour in the dry white wine, stirring continuously until the wine is mostly absorbed by the rice.

Begin Adding Broth:

- Start adding the warm vegetable or chicken broth, one ladle at a time, to the rice. Stir frequently and allow the liquid to be absorbed before adding more.

Continue Cooking:
- Continue adding broth and stirring until the rice is creamy and cooked to al dente, usually around 18-20 minutes.

Finish with Butter and Parmesan:
- Remove the skillet from heat. Stir in the remaining 1 tablespoon of butter and the grated Parmesan cheese (if using). Mix until well combined.

Season and Serve:
- Season the risotto with salt and pepper to taste.

Garnish with Fresh Parsley:
- Garnish with chopped fresh parsley. Serve the Wild Mushroom Risotto warm.

Enjoy the rich and complex flavors of wild mushrooms in this comforting and satisfying risotto. It's a perfect dish for mushroom lovers and makes for an elegant meal for special occasions.

Lemon and Dill Risotto

Ingredients:

- 1 1/2 cups Arborio rice
- 1/2 cup dry white wine
- 4 cups vegetable or chicken broth, kept warm
- Zest of 1 lemon
- Juice of 1 lemon
- 2 tablespoons fresh dill, chopped
- 1 small onion, finely chopped
- 2 cloves garlic, minced
- 2 tablespoons olive oil
- 2 tablespoons unsalted butter
- 1/2 cup Parmesan cheese, grated (optional for a non-vegan version)
- Salt and pepper, to taste
- Lemon slices and additional dill (for garnish)

Instructions:

Warm Broth:
- Heat the vegetable or chicken broth in a saucepan and keep it warm over low heat.

Sauté Onion and Garlic:
- In a large, heavy-bottomed skillet or pan, heat 1 tablespoon of butter and 1 tablespoon of olive oil over medium heat. Add the finely chopped onion and sauté until translucent. Add the minced garlic and cook for an additional 1-2 minutes.

Add Rice:
- Add the Arborio rice to the pan and cook for about 2 minutes, stirring constantly, until the rice is lightly toasted.

Deglaze with Wine:
- Pour in the dry white wine, stirring continuously until the wine is mostly absorbed by the rice.

Begin Adding Broth:
- Start adding the warm vegetable or chicken broth, one ladle at a time, to the rice. Stir frequently and allow the liquid to be absorbed before adding more.

Continue Cooking:

- Continue adding broth and stirring until the rice is creamy and cooked to al dente, usually around 18-20 minutes.

Add Lemon Zest and Juice:
- Once the rice is almost cooked, stir in the lemon zest and lemon juice. Mix well to incorporate the citrus flavors.

Fold in Dill:
- Add the chopped fresh dill to the risotto. Mix gently until the dill is evenly distributed.

Finish with Butter and Parmesan:
- Remove the skillet from heat. Stir in the remaining 1 tablespoon of butter and the grated Parmesan cheese (if using). Mix until well combined.

Season and Serve:
- Season the risotto with salt and pepper to taste.

Garnish:
- Garnish the Lemon and Dill Risotto with lemon slices and additional fresh dill.

Enjoy the bright and herby flavors of lemon and dill in this light and refreshing risotto. It's a perfect dish for spring or summer, bringing a burst of citrus and aromatic herbs to your table.

Leek and Gruyère Risotto

Ingredients:

- 1 1/2 cups Arborio rice
- 1/2 cup dry white wine
- 4 cups vegetable or chicken broth, kept warm
- 2 leeks, cleaned and thinly sliced (white and light green parts only)
- 1 cup Gruyère cheese, shredded
- 1 small onion, finely chopped
- 2 cloves garlic, minced
- 2 tablespoons olive oil
- 2 tablespoons unsalted butter
- Salt and pepper, to taste
- Fresh chives, chopped (for garnish)

Instructions:

Warm Broth:
- Heat the vegetable or chicken broth in a saucepan and keep it warm over low heat.

Sauté Leeks:
- In a large, heavy-bottomed skillet or pan, heat 1 tablespoon of butter and 1 tablespoon of olive oil over medium heat. Add the sliced leeks and sauté until they become soft and slightly caramelized, about 5-7 minutes. Remove a portion for garnish if desired.

Sauté Onion and Garlic:
- Add the finely chopped onion to the pan with the leeks. Sauté until the onion is translucent, and then add the minced garlic. Cook for an additional 1-2 minutes.

Add Rice:
- Add the Arborio rice to the pan and cook for about 2 minutes, stirring constantly, until the rice is lightly toasted.

Deglaze with Wine:
- Pour in the dry white wine, stirring continuously until the wine is mostly absorbed by the rice.

Begin Adding Broth:

- Start adding the warm vegetable or chicken broth, one ladle at a time, to the rice. Stir frequently and allow the liquid to be absorbed before adding more.

Continue Cooking:
- Continue adding broth and stirring until the rice is creamy and cooked to al dente, usually around 18-20 minutes.

Fold in Gruyère:
- Once the rice is almost cooked, fold in the shredded Gruyère cheese. Mix gently until the cheese is melted and well incorporated.

Finish with Butter:
- Remove the skillet from heat. Stir in the remaining 1 tablespoon of butter. Mix until well combined.

Season and Serve:
- Season the risotto with salt and pepper to taste.

Garnish with Leeks and Chives:
- Garnish the Leek and Gruyère Risotto with the sautéed leeks set aside earlier and chopped fresh chives.

Enjoy the creamy and cheesy goodness of Leek and Gruyère Risotto. The combination of leeks and Gruyère adds a depth of flavor that makes this risotto a comforting and satisfying dish.

Fig and Prosciutto Risotto

Ingredients:

- 1 1/2 cups Arborio rice
- 1/2 cup dry white wine
- 4 cups vegetable or chicken broth, kept warm
- 1 cup fresh figs, quartered
- 4 slices prosciutto, chopped
- 1 small onion, finely chopped
- 2 cloves garlic, minced
- 2 tablespoons olive oil
- 2 tablespoons unsalted butter
- 1/2 cup Parmesan cheese, grated (optional for a non-vegan version)
- Salt and pepper, to taste
- Fresh basil, chopped (for garnish)

Instructions:

Warm Broth:
- Heat the vegetable or chicken broth in a saucepan and keep it warm over low heat.

Sauté Onion and Garlic:
- In a large, heavy-bottomed skillet or pan, heat 1 tablespoon of butter and 1 tablespoon of olive oil over medium heat. Add the finely chopped onion and sauté until translucent. Add the minced garlic and cook for an additional 1-2 minutes.

Add Rice:
- Add the Arborio rice to the pan and cook for about 2 minutes, stirring constantly, until the rice is lightly toasted.

Deglaze with Wine:
- Pour in the dry white wine, stirring continuously until the wine is mostly absorbed by the rice.

Begin Adding Broth:
- Start adding the warm vegetable or chicken broth, one ladle at a time, to the rice. Stir frequently and allow the liquid to be absorbed before adding more.

Continue Cooking:

- Continue adding broth and stirring until the rice is creamy and cooked to al dente, usually around 18-20 minutes.

Fold in Figs and Prosciutto:
- Once the rice is almost cooked, fold in the quartered fresh figs and the chopped prosciutto. Mix gently to incorporate the figs and prosciutto into the risotto.

Finish with Butter and Parmesan:
- Remove the skillet from heat. Stir in the remaining 1 tablespoon of butter and the grated Parmesan cheese (if using). Mix until well combined.

Season and Serve:
- Season the risotto with salt and pepper to taste.

Garnish with Fresh Basil:
- Garnish the Fig and Prosciutto Risotto with chopped fresh basil.

Enjoy the sweet and salty combination of figs and prosciutto in this unique and flavorful risotto. It's a sophisticated dish that's perfect for a special occasion or to impress guests with its elegant taste and presentation.

Roquefort and Pear Risotto

Ingredients:

- 1 1/2 cups Arborio rice
- 1/2 cup dry white wine
- 4 cups vegetable or chicken broth, kept warm
- 2 ripe pears, peeled, cored, and diced
- 1 cup Roquefort cheese, crumbled
- 1 small onion, finely chopped
- 2 cloves garlic, minced
- 2 tablespoons olive oil
- 2 tablespoons unsalted butter
- Salt and pepper, to taste
- Chopped fresh thyme or parsley (for garnish)

Instructions:

Warm Broth:
- Heat the vegetable or chicken broth in a saucepan and keep it warm over low heat.

Sauté Onion and Garlic:
- In a large, heavy-bottomed skillet or pan, heat 1 tablespoon of butter and 1 tablespoon of olive oil over medium heat. Add the finely chopped onion and sauté until translucent. Add the minced garlic and cook for an additional 1-2 minutes.

Add Rice:
- Add the Arborio rice to the pan and cook for about 2 minutes, stirring constantly, until the rice is lightly toasted.

Deglaze with Wine:
- Pour in the dry white wine, stirring continuously until the wine is mostly absorbed by the rice.

Begin Adding Broth:
- Start adding the warm vegetable or chicken broth, one ladle at a time, to the rice. Stir frequently and allow the liquid to be absorbed before adding more.

Continue Cooking:

- Continue adding broth and stirring until the rice is creamy and cooked to al dente, usually around 18-20 minutes.

Fold in Pears and Roquefort:
- Once the rice is almost cooked, fold in the diced ripe pears and the crumbled Roquefort cheese. Mix gently to incorporate the pears and cheese into the risotto.

Finish with Butter:
- Remove the skillet from heat. Stir in the remaining 1 tablespoon of butter. Mix until well combined.

Season and Serve:
- Season the risotto with salt and pepper to taste.

Garnish with Fresh Thyme or Parsley:
- Garnish the Roquefort and Pear Risotto with chopped fresh thyme or parsley.

Enjoy the luxurious combination of Roquefort cheese and sweet pears in this elegant risotto. The contrasting flavors create a harmonious and delightful dish that's perfect for a special dinner or when you want to impress with a gourmet touch.

Champagne Risotto

Ingredients:

- 1 1/2 cups Arborio rice
- 1/2 cup dry champagne or sparkling wine
- 4 cups vegetable or chicken broth, kept warm
- 1 small shallot, finely chopped
- 2 tablespoons unsalted butter
- 2 tablespoons olive oil
- 1/2 cup Parmesan cheese, grated
- Salt and pepper, to taste
- Fresh chives or parsley, chopped (for garnish)

Instructions:

Warm Broth:
- Heat the vegetable or chicken broth in a saucepan and keep it warm over low heat.

Sauté Shallot:
- In a large, heavy-bottomed skillet or pan, heat 1 tablespoon of butter and 1 tablespoon of olive oil over medium heat. Add the finely chopped shallot and sauté until translucent.

Add Rice:
- Add the Arborio rice to the pan and cook for about 2 minutes, stirring constantly, until the rice is lightly toasted.

Deglaze with Champagne:
- Pour in the dry champagne or sparkling wine, stirring continuously until the liquid is mostly absorbed by the rice.

Begin Adding Broth:
- Start adding the warm vegetable or chicken broth, one ladle at a time, to the rice. Stir frequently and allow the liquid to be absorbed before adding more.

Continue Cooking:
- Continue adding broth and stirring until the rice is creamy and cooked to al dente, usually around 18-20 minutes.

Finish with Butter and Parmesan:

- When the rice is almost cooked, stir in the remaining 1 tablespoon of butter and the grated Parmesan cheese. Mix until well combined.

Season and Serve:
- Season the risotto with salt and pepper to taste.

Garnish with Fresh Herbs:
- Garnish the Champagne Risotto with chopped fresh chives or parsley.

Serve the Champagne Risotto immediately, and enjoy the rich and sophisticated flavors that the champagne brings to this classic Italian dish. This dish is perfect for celebrating special occasions or when you want to add a touch of elegance to your meal.

Walnut and Gorgonzola Risotto

Ingredients:

- 1 1/2 cups Arborio rice
- 1/2 cup dry white wine
- 4 cups vegetable or chicken broth, kept warm
- 1 cup Gorgonzola cheese, crumbled
- 1/2 cup walnuts, toasted and chopped
- 1 small onion, finely chopped
- 2 cloves garlic, minced
- 2 tablespoons olive oil
- 2 tablespoons unsalted butter
- Salt and pepper, to taste
- Fresh parsley, chopped (for garnish)

Instructions:

Warm Broth:
- Heat the vegetable or chicken broth in a saucepan and keep it warm over low heat.

Sauté Onion and Garlic:
- In a large, heavy-bottomed skillet or pan, heat 1 tablespoon of butter and 1 tablespoon of olive oil over medium heat. Add the finely chopped onion and sauté until translucent. Add the minced garlic and cook for an additional 1-2 minutes.

Add Rice:
- Add the Arborio rice to the pan and cook for about 2 minutes, stirring constantly, until the rice is lightly toasted.

Deglaze with Wine:
- Pour in the dry white wine, stirring continuously until the wine is mostly absorbed by the rice.

Begin Adding Broth:
- Start adding the warm vegetable or chicken broth, one ladle at a time, to the rice. Stir frequently and allow the liquid to be absorbed before adding more.

Continue Cooking:

- Continue adding broth and stirring until the rice is creamy and cooked to al dente, usually around 18-20 minutes.

Fold in Gorgonzola and Walnuts:
- Once the rice is almost cooked, fold in the crumbled Gorgonzola cheese and the toasted, chopped walnuts. Mix gently to incorporate the cheese and walnuts into the risotto.

Finish with Butter:
- Remove the skillet from heat. Stir in the remaining 1 tablespoon of butter. Mix until well combined.

Season and Serve:
- Season the risotto with salt and pepper to taste.

Garnish with Fresh Parsley:
- Garnish the Walnut and Gorgonzola Risotto with chopped fresh parsley.

Enjoy the rich and nutty flavor of walnuts combined with the creamy and tangy goodness of Gorgonzola cheese in this comforting and indulgent risotto. It's a perfect dish for those who appreciate the unique and bold flavors of Gorgonzola.

Sage and Pumpkin Risotto

Ingredients:

- 1 1/2 cups Arborio rice
- 1/2 cup dry white wine
- 4 cups vegetable or chicken broth, kept warm
- 1 cup pumpkin puree
- 1/2 cup Parmesan cheese, grated
- 1 small onion, finely chopped
- 2 cloves garlic, minced
- 2 tablespoons olive oil
- 2 tablespoons unsalted butter
- 1 tablespoon fresh sage, chopped
- Salt and pepper, to taste
- Nutmeg, grated (optional, for extra flavor)
- Toasted pumpkin seeds (pepitas), for garnish

Instructions:

Warm Broth:
- Heat the vegetable or chicken broth in a saucepan and keep it warm over low heat.

Sauté Onion and Garlic:
- In a large, heavy-bottomed skillet or pan, heat 1 tablespoon of butter and 1 tablespoon of olive oil over medium heat. Add the finely chopped onion and sauté until translucent. Add the minced garlic and cook for an additional 1-2 minutes.

Add Rice:
- Add the Arborio rice to the pan and cook for about 2 minutes, stirring constantly, until the rice is lightly toasted.

Deglaze with Wine:
- Pour in the dry white wine, stirring continuously until the wine is mostly absorbed by the rice.

Begin Adding Broth:
- Start adding the warm vegetable or chicken broth, one ladle at a time, to the rice. Stir frequently and allow the liquid to be absorbed before adding more.

Continue Cooking:
- Continue adding broth and stirring until the rice is creamy and cooked to al dente, usually around 18-20 minutes.

Fold in Pumpkin Puree and Sage:
- Once the rice is almost cooked, fold in the pumpkin puree and chopped fresh sage. Mix gently to incorporate the pumpkin and sage into the risotto.

Finish with Butter and Parmesan:
- Remove the skillet from heat. Stir in the remaining 1 tablespoon of butter and the grated Parmesan cheese. Mix until well combined.

Season and Serve:
- Season the risotto with salt, pepper, and grated nutmeg (if using) to taste.

Garnish with Toasted Pumpkin Seeds:
- Serve the Sage and Pumpkin Risotto warm, garnished with toasted pumpkin seeds.

Enjoy the comforting and seasonal flavors of sage and pumpkin in this creamy and hearty risotto. It's a perfect dish to celebrate fall and makes for a satisfying meal on chilly evenings.

Arugula and Pine Nut Risotto

Ingredients:

- 1 1/2 cups Arborio rice
- 1/2 cup dry white wine
- 4 cups vegetable or chicken broth, kept warm
- 2 cups fresh arugula, chopped
- 1/2 cup pine nuts, toasted
- 1 small onion, finely chopped
- 2 cloves garlic, minced
- 2 tablespoons olive oil
- 2 tablespoons unsalted butter
- 1/2 cup Parmesan cheese, grated
- Salt and pepper, to taste
- Lemon zest (optional, for extra freshness)
- Extra Parmesan cheese for serving

Instructions:

Warm Broth:
- Heat the vegetable or chicken broth in a saucepan and keep it warm over low heat.

Sauté Onion and Garlic:
- In a large, heavy-bottomed skillet or pan, heat 1 tablespoon of butter and 1 tablespoon of olive oil over medium heat. Add the finely chopped onion and sauté until translucent. Add the minced garlic and cook for an additional 1-2 minutes.

Add Rice:
- Add the Arborio rice to the pan and cook for about 2 minutes, stirring constantly, until the rice is lightly toasted.

Deglaze with Wine:
- Pour in the dry white wine, stirring continuously until the wine is mostly absorbed by the rice.

Begin Adding Broth:
- Start adding the warm vegetable or chicken broth, one ladle at a time, to the rice. Stir frequently and allow the liquid to be absorbed before adding more.

Continue Cooking:
- Continue adding broth and stirring until the rice is creamy and cooked to al dente, usually around 18-20 minutes.

Fold in Arugula and Pine Nuts:
- Once the rice is almost cooked, fold in the chopped fresh arugula and the toasted pine nuts. Mix gently to incorporate the arugula and pine nuts into the risotto.

Finish with Butter and Parmesan:
- Remove the skillet from heat. Stir in the remaining 1 tablespoon of butter and the grated Parmesan cheese. Mix until well combined.

Season and Serve:
- Season the risotto with salt and pepper to taste. If desired, add lemon zest for an extra burst of freshness.

Serve with Extra Parmesan:
- Serve the Arugula and Pine Nut Risotto warm, and offer extra Parmesan cheese on the side for individual servings.

Enjoy the vibrant flavors and textures of arugula and pine nuts in this delicious and satisfying risotto. It's a perfect dish for those who appreciate the peppery kick of arugula and the nutty richness of pine nuts.

Orange and Almond Risotto

Ingredients:

- 1 1/2 cups Arborio rice
- 1/2 cup dry white wine
- 4 cups vegetable or chicken broth, kept warm
- Zest of 2 oranges
- Juice of 1 orange
- 1/2 cup almonds, toasted and chopped
- 1 small onion, finely chopped
- 2 cloves garlic, minced
- 2 tablespoons olive oil
- 2 tablespoons unsalted butter
- 1/2 cup Parmesan cheese, grated
- Salt and pepper, to taste
- Fresh basil or mint, chopped (for garnish)

Instructions:

Warm Broth:
- Heat the vegetable or chicken broth in a saucepan and keep it warm over low heat.

Sauté Onion and Garlic:
- In a large, heavy-bottomed skillet or pan, heat 1 tablespoon of butter and 1 tablespoon of olive oil over medium heat. Add the finely chopped onion and sauté until translucent. Add the minced garlic and cook for an additional 1-2 minutes.

Add Rice:
- Add the Arborio rice to the pan and cook for about 2 minutes, stirring constantly, until the rice is lightly toasted.

Deglaze with Wine:
- Pour in the dry white wine, stirring continuously until the wine is mostly absorbed by the rice.

Begin Adding Broth:
- Start adding the warm vegetable or chicken broth, one ladle at a time, to the rice. Stir frequently and allow the liquid to be absorbed before adding more.

Continue Cooking:
- Continue adding broth and stirring until the rice is creamy and cooked to al dente, usually around 18-20 minutes.

Fold in Orange Zest and Juice:
- Once the rice is almost cooked, fold in the orange zest and juice. Mix gently to incorporate the citrusy flavors into the risotto.

Fold in Toasted Almonds:
- Add the toasted and chopped almonds to the risotto. Mix gently to incorporate the almonds and add a nutty crunch.

Finish with Butter and Parmesan:
- Remove the skillet from heat. Stir in the remaining 1 tablespoon of butter and the grated Parmesan cheese. Mix until well combined.

Season and Serve:
- Season the Orange and Almond Risotto with salt and pepper to taste.

Garnish with Fresh Basil or Mint:
- Garnish the risotto with chopped fresh basil or mint.

Enjoy the bright and refreshing combination of orange and almond in this unique and flavorful risotto. It's a perfect dish to add a burst of citrusy goodness to your dinner table.

Pecorino and Black Pepper Risotto

Ingredients:

- 1 1/2 cups Arborio rice
- 1/2 cup dry white wine
- 4 cups vegetable or chicken broth, kept warm
- 1 1/2 cups Pecorino Romano cheese, grated
- Freshly ground black pepper, to taste
- 1 small onion, finely chopped
- 2 cloves garlic, minced
- 2 tablespoons olive oil
- 2 tablespoons unsalted butter
- Salt, to taste
- Fresh parsley, chopped (for garnish)

Instructions:

Warm Broth:
- Heat the vegetable or chicken broth in a saucepan and keep it warm over low heat.

Sauté Onion and Garlic:
- In a large, heavy-bottomed skillet or pan, heat 1 tablespoon of butter and 1 tablespoon of olive oil over medium heat. Add the finely chopped onion and sauté until translucent. Add the minced garlic and cook for an additional 1-2 minutes.

Add Rice:
- Add the Arborio rice to the pan and cook for about 2 minutes, stirring constantly, until the rice is lightly toasted.

Deglaze with Wine:
- Pour in the dry white wine, stirring continuously until the wine is mostly absorbed by the rice.

Begin Adding Broth:
- Start adding the warm vegetable or chicken broth, one ladle at a time, to the rice. Stir frequently and allow the liquid to be absorbed before adding more.

Continue Cooking:

- Continue adding broth and stirring until the rice is creamy and cooked to al dente, usually around 18-20 minutes.

Fold in Pecorino and Black Pepper:
- Once the rice is almost cooked, fold in the grated Pecorino Romano cheese and freshly ground black pepper. Mix gently to incorporate the cheese and pepper into the risotto.

Finish with Butter:
- Remove the skillet from heat. Stir in the remaining 1 tablespoon of butter. Mix until well combined.

Season and Serve:
- Taste the risotto and adjust the salt if necessary.

Garnish with Fresh Parsley:
- Garnish the Pecorino and Black Pepper Risotto with chopped fresh parsley.

Enjoy the simplicity and bold flavors of this classic Roman dish. The combination of Pecorino and black pepper creates a rich and savory risotto that's both comforting and satisfying. Serve it warm and freshly prepared for the best experience.

Basil and Pine Nut Risotto

Ingredients:

- 1 1/2 cups Arborio rice
- 1/2 cup dry white wine
- 4 cups vegetable or chicken broth, kept warm
- 1 cup fresh basil leaves, chopped
- 1/2 cup pine nuts, toasted
- 1 small onion, finely chopped
- 2 cloves garlic, minced
- 2 tablespoons olive oil
- 2 tablespoons unsalted butter
- 1/2 cup Parmesan cheese, grated
- Salt and pepper, to taste
- Lemon zest (optional, for extra brightness)

Instructions:

Warm Broth:
- Heat the vegetable or chicken broth in a saucepan and keep it warm over low heat.

Sauté Onion and Garlic:
- In a large, heavy-bottomed skillet or pan, heat 1 tablespoon of butter and 1 tablespoon of olive oil over medium heat. Add the finely chopped onion and sauté until translucent. Add the minced garlic and cook for an additional 1-2 minutes.

Add Rice:
- Add the Arborio rice to the pan and cook for about 2 minutes, stirring constantly, until the rice is lightly toasted.

Deglaze with Wine:
- Pour in the dry white wine, stirring continuously until the wine is mostly absorbed by the rice.

Begin Adding Broth:
- Start adding the warm vegetable or chicken broth, one ladle at a time, to the rice. Stir frequently and allow the liquid to be absorbed before adding more.

Continue Cooking:

- Continue adding broth and stirring until the rice is creamy and cooked to al dente, usually around 18-20 minutes.

Fold in Basil and Pine Nuts:
- Once the rice is almost cooked, fold in the chopped fresh basil and the toasted pine nuts. Mix gently to incorporate the basil and pine nuts into the risotto.

Finish with Butter and Parmesan:
- Remove the skillet from heat. Stir in the remaining 1 tablespoon of butter and the grated Parmesan cheese. Mix until well combined.

Season and Serve:
- Season the Basil and Pine Nut Risotto with salt and pepper to taste. If desired, add lemon zest for extra brightness.

Serve Warm:
- Spoon the risotto into serving dishes and serve warm.

Enjoy the aromatic and nutty goodness of basil and pine nuts in this delicious risotto. It's a perfect dish to celebrate the fresh flavors of summer or to add a burst of herbaceousness to your meal.

Blue Cheese and Pear Risotto

Ingredients:

- 1 1/2 cups Arborio rice
- 1/2 cup dry white wine
- 4 cups vegetable or chicken broth, kept warm
- 1 cup blue cheese, crumbled (choose a variety you enjoy)
- 2 ripe pears, peeled, cored, and diced
- 1 small onion, finely chopped
- 2 cloves garlic, minced
- 2 tablespoons olive oil
- 2 tablespoons unsalted butter
- Salt and pepper, to taste
- Fresh thyme leaves, for garnish

Instructions:

Warm Broth:
- Heat the vegetable or chicken broth in a saucepan and keep it warm over low heat.

Sauté Onion and Garlic:
- In a large, heavy-bottomed skillet or pan, heat 1 tablespoon of butter and 1 tablespoon of olive oil over medium heat. Add the finely chopped onion and sauté until translucent. Add the minced garlic and cook for an additional 1-2 minutes.

Add Rice:
- Add the Arborio rice to the pan and cook for about 2 minutes, stirring constantly, until the rice is lightly toasted.

Deglaze with Wine:
- Pour in the dry white wine, stirring continuously until the wine is mostly absorbed by the rice.

Begin Adding Broth:
- Start adding the warm vegetable or chicken broth, one ladle at a time, to the rice. Stir frequently and allow the liquid to be absorbed before adding more.

Continue Cooking:

- Continue adding broth and stirring until the rice is creamy and cooked to al dente, usually around 18-20 minutes.

Fold in Blue Cheese and Pears:
- Once the rice is almost cooked, fold in the crumbled blue cheese and the diced ripe pears. Mix gently to incorporate the blue cheese and pears into the risotto.

Finish with Butter:
- Remove the skillet from heat. Stir in the remaining 1 tablespoon of butter. Mix until well combined.

Season and Serve:
- Season the Blue Cheese and Pear Risotto with salt and pepper to taste.

Garnish with Fresh Thyme:
- Serve the risotto warm, garnished with fresh thyme leaves.

Enjoy the exquisite combination of creamy blue cheese and sweet pears in this sophisticated risotto. It's a perfect dish for a special occasion or when you want to impress with a unique and delicious flavor pairing.

Smoked Trout Risotto

Ingredients:

- 1 1/2 cups Arborio rice
- 1/2 cup dry white wine
- 4 cups fish or vegetable broth, kept warm
- 200g smoked trout, flaked
- 1 small onion, finely chopped
- 2 cloves garlic, minced
- 2 tablespoons olive oil
- 2 tablespoons unsalted butter
- 1/2 cup Parmesan cheese, grated
- Zest of 1 lemon
- Juice of half a lemon
- Salt and pepper, to taste
- Fresh dill, chopped (for garnish)

Instructions:

Warm Broth:
- Heat the fish or vegetable broth in a saucepan and keep it warm over low heat.

Sauté Onion and Garlic:
- In a large, heavy-bottomed skillet or pan, heat 1 tablespoon of butter and 1 tablespoon of olive oil over medium heat. Add the finely chopped onion and sauté until translucent. Add the minced garlic and cook for an additional 1-2 minutes.

Add Rice:
- Add the Arborio rice to the pan and cook for about 2 minutes, stirring constantly, until the rice is lightly toasted.

Deglaze with Wine:
- Pour in the dry white wine, stirring continuously until the wine is mostly absorbed by the rice.

Begin Adding Broth:
- Start adding the warm fish or vegetable broth, one ladle at a time, to the rice. Stir frequently and allow the liquid to be absorbed before adding more.

Continue Cooking:

- Continue adding broth and stirring until the rice is creamy and cooked to al dente, usually around 18-20 minutes.

Fold in Smoked Trout:
- Once the rice is almost cooked, fold in the flaked smoked trout. Mix gently to incorporate the smoky flavor into the risotto.

Finish with Butter and Parmesan:
- Remove the skillet from heat. Stir in the remaining 1 tablespoon of butter and the grated Parmesan cheese. Mix until well combined.

Add Lemon Zest and Juice:
- Stir in the lemon zest and juice. Adjust the seasoning with salt and pepper to taste.

Garnish with Fresh Dill:
- Serve the Smoked Trout Risotto warm, garnished with chopped fresh dill.

Enjoy the rich and smoky flavors of smoked trout in this luxurious risotto. The addition of lemon zest and juice adds a refreshing twist, and the fresh dill complements the dish with a burst of herbaceousness. Serve it as a main course for a special dinner or as an impressive appetizer.

Walnut and Cranberry Risotto

Ingredients:

- 1 1/2 cups Arborio rice
- 1/2 cup dry white wine
- 4 cups vegetable or chicken broth, kept warm
- 1 cup walnuts, chopped and toasted
- 1/2 cup dried cranberries
- 1 small onion, finely chopped
- 2 cloves garlic, minced
- 2 tablespoons olive oil
- 2 tablespoons unsalted butter
- 1/2 cup Parmesan cheese, grated
- Salt and pepper, to taste
- Fresh parsley, chopped (for garnish)

Instructions:

Warm Broth:
- Heat the vegetable or chicken broth in a saucepan and keep it warm over low heat.

Sauté Onion and Garlic:
- In a large, heavy-bottomed skillet or pan, heat 1 tablespoon of butter and 1 tablespoon of olive oil over medium heat. Add the finely chopped onion and sauté until translucent. Add the minced garlic and cook for an additional 1-2 minutes.

Add Rice:
- Add the Arborio rice to the pan and cook for about 2 minutes, stirring constantly, until the rice is lightly toasted.

Deglaze with Wine:
- Pour in the dry white wine, stirring continuously until the wine is mostly absorbed by the rice.

Begin Adding Broth:
- Start adding the warm vegetable or chicken broth, one ladle at a time, to the rice. Stir frequently and allow the liquid to be absorbed before adding more.

Continue Cooking:

- Continue adding broth and stirring until the rice is creamy and cooked to al dente, usually around 18-20 minutes.

Fold in Walnuts and Cranberries:
- Once the rice is almost cooked, fold in the chopped and toasted walnuts and the dried cranberries. Mix gently to incorporate the walnuts and cranberries into the risotto.

Finish with Butter and Parmesan:
- Remove the skillet from heat. Stir in the remaining 1 tablespoon of butter and the grated Parmesan cheese. Mix until well combined.

Season and Serve:
- Season the Walnut and Cranberry Risotto with salt and pepper to taste.

Garnish with Fresh Parsley:
- Serve the risotto warm, garnished with chopped fresh parsley.

Enjoy the comforting and festive combination of walnuts and cranberries in this delicious risotto. It's a perfect dish for the holiday season or any time you want a flavorful and satisfying meal.

Buttermilk and Lemon Risotto

Ingredients:

- 1 1/2 cups Arborio rice
- 1/2 cup dry white wine
- 4 cups vegetable or chicken broth, kept warm
- 1 cup buttermilk
- Zest of 2 lemons
- Juice of 1 lemon
- 1 small onion, finely chopped
- 2 cloves garlic, minced
- 2 tablespoons olive oil
- 2 tablespoons unsalted butter
- 1/2 cup Parmesan cheese, grated
- Salt and pepper, to taste
- Fresh chives, chopped (for garnish)

Instructions:

Warm Broth:
- Heat the vegetable or chicken broth in a saucepan and keep it warm over low heat.

Sauté Onion and Garlic:
- In a large, heavy-bottomed skillet or pan, heat 1 tablespoon of butter and 1 tablespoon of olive oil over medium heat. Add the finely chopped onion and sauté until translucent. Add the minced garlic and cook for an additional 1-2 minutes.

Add Rice:
- Add the Arborio rice to the pan and cook for about 2 minutes, stirring constantly, until the rice is lightly toasted.

Deglaze with Wine:
- Pour in the dry white wine, stirring continuously until the wine is mostly absorbed by the rice.

Begin Adding Broth:
- Start adding the warm vegetable or chicken broth, one ladle at a time, to the rice. Stir frequently and allow the liquid to be absorbed before adding more.

Continue Cooking:
- Continue adding broth and stirring until the rice is creamy and cooked to al dente, usually around 18-20 minutes.

Fold in Buttermilk and Lemon:
- Once the rice is almost cooked, fold in the buttermilk, lemon zest, and lemon juice. Mix gently to incorporate the tangy flavors into the risotto.

Finish with Butter and Parmesan:
- Remove the skillet from heat. Stir in the remaining 1 tablespoon of butter and the grated Parmesan cheese. Mix until well combined.

Season and Serve:
- Season the Buttermilk and Lemon Risotto with salt and pepper to taste.

Garnish with Fresh Chives:
- Serve the risotto warm, garnished with chopped fresh chives.

Enjoy the creamy and citrusy goodness of buttermilk and lemon in this refreshing risotto. It's a perfect dish for spring or summer, bringing a light and tangy twist to the classic Italian comfort food.

www.ingramcontent.com/pod-product-compliance
Lightning Source LLC
LaVergne TN
LVHW081600060526
838201LV00054B/1994